Journeys

JOURNEYS

JAN MORRIS

New York   Oxford
OXFORD UNIVERSITY PRESS
1984

Copyright © 1984 by Jan Morris

Library of Congress Cataloging in Publication Data
Morris, Jan, 1926–
Journeys.
1. Morris, Jan, 1926– .
2. Voyages and travels—1951– . I. Title.
G465.M66   1984   910.4   83-25009
ISBN 0-19-503452-X

The essays in this book appeared in slightly different form in the following publica-
tions: "The Best of Everything—Stockholm, Sweden" in *Connoisseur*, New York;
"Not So Far—A European Journey" in *Encounter*, London; "In Ruritania—Cetinje,
Yugoslavia" in *Geo*, New York; "Boomtown!—Houston, U.S.A." and "Trans-Texan—
An American Journey" in *Texas Monthly*, Austin; "A Visit to Barchester—Wells,
England" and "Oil on Granite—Aberdeen, Scotland" in *The Times*, London; all
other essays first appeared in *Rolling Stone*, New York.

Printed in the United States of America

INTRODUCTORY

This collection is rather in the nature of a mystery tour, when you make your booking without knowing your destination. It describes a jumbled succession of journeys offered without benefit of itinerary, some to places far away and exotic, some to places more familiar.

Their only unity is a unity of time, for they are nearly all journeys of the early 1980s. It has been a bewildering decade so far—ominous, too—so perhaps it is only proper that such a contemporary expedition should promise no certainty of a ticket home!

Trefan Morys, 1984   J.M.

CONTENTS

Journeys

Over the Bridge

AN AUSTRALIAN JOURNEY

K ev. *Kev!* Time you got going."
  "Jeez, Sandra, it's raining out there."

"TV says it's fining up. You're not crook are you, Kev? It's all that booze
you know, Kev, you know what the doctor said, cut down on the booze,
he said, no wonder you're crook in the mornings, the human body can
take only so much. . . ."

But Kev has slipped out by now, and with his office gear slung in his
backpack is away, and up the steps, and halfway along the approach to
the great bridge.

If he was crook, he is crook no more, for the TV was right, the rain
clears as if by magic, and all the glory of the winter morning unfolds
over the water as he breaks into his jog along the sidewalk. He is joining
the stream of life itself! To his right the suburban trains clatter, the commuter cars lurch in fits and starts towards the city. To his left ferries
bustle across the harbor, the first hydrofoil is streaking in a foamy curve
towards the sea, the very first yacht is slipping from its moorings, and a
tug is on its way, riding lights still burning, to meet the towering freighter
just appearing around the headland.

On the harbor bridge there are already plenty of people about. He
overtakes briskly walking businessmen with briefcases and identical
moustaches. He is overtaken by huge athletes in sweatbands and sloganed
shirts. Archetypal schoolboys loiter their way, satchels dangling, reluc-
tantly towards their education. An elderly lady in a mackintosh cries

"Grand to see the sun again!" in an exaggeratedly Irish brogue. Another pack of giants comes panting and sweating past. Another covey of schoolboys kicks a pebble here and there. Ahead of him, between the massive pylons of the bridge, the city towers are beginning to gleam in the sun, and there is a flashing of upper windows, and a fluttering of flags in and out of shadow, and a golden shine from the observation deck of the tallest tower of all.

It is as though the innocence of the morning has infected the whole scene, and made everything young. A pristine vigor is on the air, very fresh and good for you, like orange juice. By the time Kev reaches his office on the 17th floor, he feels he's never drunk a tinny of Foster's in his life: and looking back upon the scurrying ferries of the Circular Quay, the flying white roofs of the Opera House, the traffic still streaming across the bridge, the rising sun and the water and the green parklands all around, silently he congratulates himself once more, as he does every morning as a matter of principle, upon his great good fortune in being born an Australian.

$$-o\,/\,o\,/\,o-$$

The city he surveys is a very concentrate of that condition. The whole matter of Australia, history, character, reputation, attitude, finds its best epitome in this particular corner of the great land mass, where Sydney stands beside its fjord-like harbor. When the world thinks of Australia, it thinks of that bridge, that Opera House, that wake-frothed and yacht-flecked harbor. When the world thinks of an Australian, it thinks, more or less, of Kev.

Australian society is overwhelmingly urban, and Sydney is Australia *urbanissima*. Canberra is the capital, Adelaide is a delight, Perth holds the America's Cup, Melbourne people believe their city to be at least as mature, civilized and unutterably lovely, but only Sydney has the true metropolitan presence. An enormous spread of suburbia around an intensely packed downtown, it stands upon its marvellous haven in the stance of proper consequence. A glittering business quarter makes one feel it is keyed in to the Wall Street–London–Zurich–Hong Kong circuit of profit. The inescapable presence of virtually the whole Australian Navy, moored beside its dockyards or glamorously returning from sea with ensigns flying and radars twirling, gives it a front-line air. It is equipped with all the statutory metropolitan tokens—city marathon, revolving restaurant, supine veiled figure by Henry Moore, breakfast TV and Bahai temple.

Its stature really resides, though, not in its universality, not in its membership in the league of big cities, but for better or worse, like it or not, in its unchallengeable Australian-ness. It is a metropolis *sui generis*. Take its looks for a start. Architecturally Sydney is no great shakes. Its suburbs are at best pleasantly ordinary, enlivened only, here and there, by wrought iron and engaging terracing. Its downtown is handsome but unexceptional, the usual cubes, cylinders, plazas and mirror-walls of contemporary urbanism surrounding the usual clumps of nineteenth-century florid. It has no elegant set pieces of civic planning, and has crudely degraded its waterfront on Sydney Cove, the site of its beginnings and still the focus of its life, by building an expressway slap across it.

Yet it is one of the most beautiful cities in the world, specifically because it is Australian. That winding, nooky, islanded, bosky harbor thrillingly reminds one always that Sydney stands on the shore of an island totally unlike anywhere else on earth. The pale pure light of the Sydney winter seems to come straight from the bergs and ice mountains of Antarctica. The foliage of Sydney's parks and gardens is queerly drooped and tangled, apparently antediluvian fig trees overshadow suburban streets, and the perpetual passing of the ships through the very heart of the city gives everything a tingling sense of remoteness. The water goes down the plug-hole the other way in Australia, and it really is possible to imagine, if you are a fancifully-minded visitor from the other hemisphere, that this metropolis is clinging upside-down to the bottom of the earth, so subtly antipodean, or perhaps marsupial, is the nature of the scene.

The supreme Sydney experience, for such a traveller, is a walk on a brisk sunny morning around the headland called Mrs. Macquarie's Chair, through a complex of park and garden beside the harbor. Except only for Stanley Park in Vancouver, this seems to me the loveliest of all city parklands, but its loveliness is of a sly, deceptive kind. It is like a park in the mind. The grass is almost too vividly green, the trees look curiously artificial, parakeets squawk viciously at each other in the shrubbery. The shifting scene around you, as you walk the park's perimeter, seems more ideal than actual—water everywhere, and those grey warships at their quays, and glimpses of Riviera-like settlements all around, and a sham castle in a garden, and the inescapable passing of the ferries.

And slyest of all is the prospect as you round the point itself, where the families are spreading their picnics on the grass, and a solitary ibis is burrowing for edibles in a rubbish can; for there suddenly like an aery fantasy the Sydney Opera House, most peculiar of architectural masterpieces, spreads its white wings in the sunshine, light as some unsuspected waterbird, with the massive old harbor bridge, a beast to its insubstantial beauty, all brutal heft above.

−o / o / o−

Those two unforgettable structures, the one rooted so powerfully in the bedrock, the other aspiring to the state of levitation, represent the nature of this city more than aesthetically. Upon Sydney's foundation of absolute British Australian-ness has been superimposed a prismatically ethnic superstructure, making this city, formerly one of the most homogenous and stodgy in the world, a fascinating mix of the complacent and the tentative, the almost immovable and the practically irresistible.

Once it used to suggest nowhere else. Now it is full of alien allusion. It reminds me often of Stockholm. As Sydney is to the South, Stockholm is to the North, and Sydney's Australia is Stockholm's Scandinavia—I am not surprised that the Danish architect of the Opera House clearly had in his memory, as he planned his prodigy, Stockholm's Town Hall upon an inlet of another sea. The light of this southern fjord is not unlike the light of the Baltic; a pallid freshness is common to both cities; sitting snugly out of the sunlight in Sydney's Strand Arcade, all fancy balustrades and tesselated paving, sometimes I almost expect to see the shoppers shaking the snow from their galoshes, breathing in their hands to restore the circulation, and ordering themselves a schnapps.

At other moments Sydney reminds me of somewhere in Central Europe; any Saturday morning in the plush waterside suburb called Double Bay, for example, when the rich immigrants assemble in the street café of the Cosmopolitan, talking loudly in Ruritanian, or deep in the financial pages of the *Sydney Morning Herald*. Like the bourgeoisie of old Prague or Budapest they while the hours away in chat and exhibitionism—here four men with coats slung over their shoulders, smoking small cigars and passionately arguing about President Benes—here a couple of leathery ladies, furred and proudly diamonded, sitting in lofty silence over aperitifs—a young poseur in a deer-stalker hat, smoking a cigarette in a long jade holder, a gaggle of Double Bay socialites in the swathed ragbag fashion, faintly Martial Arts in suggestion, rampant in Sydney at the moment.

Lebanese proliferate in Sydney, and Greeks, and Filipinos, and Indonesians. The Vietnamese, they tell me, are shifting out of the western suburbs towards East Sydney. Maori gays, gossip picturesquely maintains, are taking over Bondi. The Spanish Club advertises itself with a picture of Don Quixote and Sancho riding out of a golden Outback. Sydney's Chinatown booms with investment from Hong Kong, and the Chinese taste for unexpectedly mixed foods seems to have infected the entire municipal cuisine, so that perfectly true-blue Aussie restaurants are likely to offer you hot buttered pumpkin and orange soup with peppercorns floating in it, or quail in a sauce made of red wine and bacon. The Sydney Municipal Board sometimes likes to announce itself in all the languages of its tax-paying citizenry—MESTSKÁ RADA SYDNEY or SYDNEY VÁVOSI TANÁCS—and these arcane proclamations, attached to some lumpish municipal pile of mid-Victorian imperialism, pungently illustrate the state of things.

Still dominant nevertheless, as the bridge looms high over the Opera House, stand the likes of Kev. The flow of immigration has softened, eased and illuminated Sydney, but it came too late ever to displace the original bloodstream of this city. Half a century ago 98 percent of Sydney people were of British descent, and it is they, the Old Australians, who still set the anthropological tone. Sit long enough among the Ruritanians at the Cosmopolitan, and some beefy young Ocker will arrive to steal the scene and drink his beer out of the bottle. Go to *La Traviata* at the Opera House, and my, what an unexpectedly hearty and robust chorus of ladies and gentlemen will be attendant upon Violetta in the opening act, their crinolines and Parisian whiskers delightfully failing to disguise physiques born out of Australian surf and sunshine, and names like Higginson and O'Rourke—while even La Traviata herself, as she subsides to the last curtain, may seem to you the victim of some specifically Australian variety of tuberculosis, since she looks as though immediately after the curtain-call she will be off for a vigorous set of tennis with the conductor, or at least a grilled lobster with orange sauce and caramel.

Such is the strength of Kev's sub-species, into which the children of all those immigrants, too, are inexorably mutated. Years ago, waiting for the Manly ferry, I caught the eye of a young Italian working at a coffee-stall, and I remember distinctly the wiry black Latinate quality of his person. I went down there again the other day to see if he was still about, and found him not just aged and plumped, but altogether altered by the Kev Effect—his face pulled' into a different shape, his sparkle replaced by something more wary or blunted, or perhaps dreamier. And when he spoke, the last traces of Neapolitanism were all but hidden beneath the virile twisted vowels of Australian English.

Language they say is the badge of nationality, and above all else it is the language of Sydney that binds this fissile society into a recondite unity. It is many years since the writer Monica Dickens, at a Sydney signing session, inscribed a volume to Emma Chissett, misunderstanding a lady who wanted to know the price of the book, but fundamentally the vernacular has not changed: "Emma Chissett?" I make a point of asking now, when I want to buy something, and the shop assistants never give me a second glance, taking my dinkum Aussiness for granted, and frequently confiding in me their grievances about the train service from Parramatta.

Or from Woop Woop perhaps, an imaginary township which has become a Sydney generic for the back of beyond. Sydney English is full of such fantasies and in-jokes, and consciously perpetuates itself in self-amusement, hardly a year passing without another new dictionary of the argot. Usages change constantly—out goes *she'll be apples* ("it'll be OK"), in comes *throwing a mental* (losing one's temper)—and there is almost nobody in Sydney, schoolboy to sage, who is not eager to discuss the present state of the vernacular. Why do Sydney women end all their sentences, even the most definite, with a rising interrogative inflection? Because they're so put down they daren't say anything for sure. What's the true definition of an Ocker? "A man who watches the footy on TV with a terry-towel hat on his head and a tinny of Foster's balanced on his belly."

The language makes the man, and makes the city too. Without his language your Sydney citizen (he no longer calls himself a Sydneysider) might be taken for a Scandinavian, a Californian or even sometimes an Englishman: with it even a second-generation immigrant can be mistaken for nobody else, and the fizz and the fun of the tongue reflects Sydney's particular strain of constancy. The pubs of this city are loud with jazz and rock music, deafening the packed saloons within, blaring over the sidewalks. Often the thump of it drives the customers into a frenzy, and the bars are full of strapping young Ockers throwing their hands above their heads, whoopeeing and beating their enormous feet. They are not at all like roisterers of Europe or America, partly because they all seem to be, like that opera chorus, in a condition of exuberant physical well-being, partly because the tang of their language pervades everything they do, and for a time I thought their burly disco to be something altogether new out of Sydney, an Australization specifically of the 1980s.

But emerging half-shattered one day from the Observer Inn, having weaved a perilous way among those flailing limbs and stomping size 14s, I chanced to see, in a shop down the road, a print of early Sydney settlers living it up 150 years ago. They wore floppy slouch hats and check shirts, were heavily bearded, and were probably celebrating their recent release from hard labor in the prisons: but they were kicking their legs about in that self-same Sydney fandango, in just the same heavyweight high jinks, and were yelling their songs and cheerful obscenities, I am sure, in similarly rank and entertaining distortions.

—o / o / o—

For even Sydney has a past. It began in the 1780s with the arrival of the first British convicts, put ashore here in their chains to serve as the reluctant and incongruous Founding Fathers of Australia. It ended in the 1950s with the mass landings of the European immigrants, disembarking after their Government-subsidized passages to transform Australia from semi-emancipated colonialism into Pacific cosmopolitanism. By then the penal colony had developed into a city of great but somewhat unlovely character, chauvinist to an almost comical degree, with an elite of often snobby and vulgar monarchists, and a labor force so powerful that unionists everywhere called this the Worker's Paradise. In those days any Sydney matron worth her social salt boasted of her distant connection with the Earl of Mudcastle, while the Sydney proletariat was as rough, as ready, as truculent, as contemptuous of Earls and as militantly Irish as a self-respecting proletariat ought to be.

Today that society has mostly gone underground. If you want a symbolic demonstration of it, try going to the subterranean railway station beside the Town Hall: for there behind the trendily creeper-covered walls of the sunken plaza, all waterfalls and canopies, the station itself survives as a very museum of the Old Australia—brass knobs, bakelite switches, Instructions to Employees in copper-plate script behind brass-framed glass, bare electric bulbs lighting up to announce the next train to Pymble or Hornby. The Sydney railways are very Old Australia. So are the ferries, and the less liberated pubs, and the memorials to kings and queens and Robbie Burns. The grand-daughters of those well-connected matrons still curtsey with a preposterous zeal when Prince Charles drops by. Go-slows on the Woop Woop line, heavy-jowled men with placards demanding a Fair Go For Aussie Ships, recall the heyday of the Worker's Paradise. The old beery machismo has not been entirely subsumed in white wine and unisex hairdressing.

More importantly, out of the Old Australia comes Sydney's sense of order and fair play, which underpins the shifting vigor of this city. "KINDNESS AND COURTESY" is still the motto of Double Bay School, and to a remarkable degree the old values obtain. You might expect this haven on a creek at the bottom of the world to be a seamy, wild and reckless place, and of course Australians, like city people everywhere on earth, talk with dismay of rising crime rates and drunken driving. By most standards, though, Sydney is good as gold. The streets are much safer than most, the traffic is generally demure enough, even jay-walkers look guilty, and the city comports itself, at least to visitors, with unfailing politesse.

These are legacies based, *au fond,* upon Parliamentary democracy and the Common Law, and their survival is a tribute to their strength: for what has happened all around them, in the last three decades, is nothing less than a social revolution. Sydney has become a different city, different in style, in aspiration, in loyalty, in taste. A generation ago, it seemed to me, the very core of the Sydney ethos was the memory of the sacrifices its men had made in the two World Wars, fighting in a cause almost quixotically remote to them, yet made poignantly real by their devotion to Crown, Flag and Empire. The heroic ordeals of Gallipoli and Alamein stood somewhere near the root of the civic pride, and the Returned Servicemen's League was sacrosanct and inescapable.

But on a recent winter Sunday I revisited the great war memorial in Hyde Park which was the shrine of those epic memories, and found its tragic magnetism dispersed. It stood there still of course, grey, powerful and sombre among the trees; the sad sculpted soldiers still looked down, sitting like thoughtful gods around the parapet; but the people in the park somehow seemed to shy away from its presence, as though it had been put out of their minds by some process of re-education, or sealed up, with all its toxic energies, like an expended reactor.

–o / o / o–

It seems only proper that the motto of another Sydney school, "I Hear, I See, I Learn," should translate into Latin as *Audio, Video, Disco,* for the young have boisterously discarded the old image of Sydney, and have re-molded it again in their own. Today this city is one of the world's great promises, a pledge of better things, living in a state of ill-defined but perpetual expectancy.

It is a very young city: not just young in manners and accomplishment, but exceedingly young in person. Sometimes indeed it seems to be in-habited chiefly by schoolchildren, children kicking pebbles across bridges, children racing fig leaves down the channels of ornamental fountains, children clambering like invading armies all over the Opera House, or mustered in their thousands in the New South Wales Art Gallery. They seem to me a stalwart crew. "Now this is a Picasso," I heard a teacher say in the gallery one day, "I'm sure you all know who Picasso was." "I don't," piped up a solitary small Australian at the back, and I bowed to him as the only absolutely honest soul in sight.

It is a city attuned to young ideas—"Barefoot shoppers," sensibly de-crees one of the grandest department stores, "must not use the escala-tors"—and its youthfulness is so pervasive as to be almost hallucinatory. The magistrate in the petty sessions court looks like a second-year law student, the prosecuting attorney might just have invested in his first motor-bike, and surely the accused, who is charged with public indecency, has not yet reached the age of puberty? As for the Stock Exchange, it ap-pears to be run by several hundred athletes, helped by a few go-go girls in miniskirts, and the old men in the public gallery upstairs, ostensibly examining the shares board through their binoculars to see how Consoli-dated Metals are doing, look to me less like speculators than plain voyeurs.

The youthfulness of Sydney, like all youthfulness, is a little schizo, be-ing half brash, but half timid. In a posh Sydney hotel, for instance, or an upstage Sydney restaurant, customers tend to behave with a detectable sense of reverence, talking in undertones to each other and gratefully ac-cepting the wine-waiter's recommendation—it would be a *maîtres d's* de-light, were it not for the fact that in Sydney even that insufferable guild behaves with a becoming inhibition. Australians always used to be ac-cused of inferiority complex, and though their image in the world is very different now, still Sydney has not reached the free fine assurance of absolute civic maturity—"When I go to California," a very attractive and intelligent Sydney girl said to me, "I feel like a mouse." And the mouse instinct erupts sometimes, of course, as it always does, into absurd expressions of self-assertion. Sydney people are far less vulnerable to criticism than they used to be—when I first wrote an article about this city, it was five full years before the last furious letter reached me—but they are hardly less sensitive to the patronizing or the aloof. In Europe, one Sydney intellectual told me severely, ignorance about Australian affairs was abysmal, *abysmal*—why in London, he had been assured, reputable art critics had never even heard of Brett Whiteley!

"Brett Who?" I could not resist inquiring (remembering the boy in the art gallery) for this aspect of the Sydney style can be a bit relentless. One is told a little too often of the Whiteley genius, one tires of the gossip about the Sidney Whites and the Patrick Nolans; yes, one did realize that the author of *Schindler's List* was a local man; for myself I feel lucky to have missed the recent Sydney fashion show, about which I heard so much, which featured a ballet performance to aboriginal msuic, songs with flute accompaniment against a background of wrecked cars, and some extreme examples of the Bundled Jap look.

But then youth, hope and silliness go together, in cities as in people, and it is the hope that counts. The hope is what Kev unconsciously feels, as he jogs over the bridge in the morning, and what nearly every stranger feels too, on a first foray into the streets of Sydney. How young and strong the city! How magnificent the promise! One forgets sometimes that even in the Land of Oz, youth is not eternal. . . .

–o / o / o–

The Reeperbahn or 42nd Street of Sydney is King's Cross, a mile or two southeast of Sydney Cove. This used to be an entertaining Bohemian quarter, but has degenerated lately into a nasty combination of squalor and pathos. Among the usual Reeperbahn company of pimps, pornographers, strippers, tattooists and transvestites, bathed in the conventionally sinful half-light, gaped at by the inevitable visitors from Woop Woop, through King's Cross after midnight there now move some more heart-rending figures: child-prostitutes, hardly in their teens, desperately made up and not very expertly soliciting the passing drunks and lechers.

John Gunther, the great reporter, used to ask, wherever he went in the world, "Who runs this place?" It is my practice to ask who (or in print, perhaps, *whom*) I ought to be sorry for. In some cities—think of Calcutta, think of Johannesburg!—the question is superfluous. In many another the tender heart is wrung by terrible poverty, or political oppression, or general gloom of environment. In Sydney there is hardly any abject poverty. Politically the people of this city are free as air, socially they are as emancipated as anyone on earth. Their town is clean and mostly safe, their climate is a dream, and though they grumble a good deal about the effects of recession, and frequently go on strike, by the standards of the world at large they live magnificently.

So who should I be sorry for? Sydney people are puzzled by the question, and sometimes can't think of anyone at all. Sometimes they reply with jokes about unsuccessful football players or politicians in eclipse. "Me," says Kev, but he does not mean it. A few propose those poor children of King's Cross, there are vague references sometimes to derelicts ("derros") or exploited immigrants. And in the end it occurs to most people that I should give a thought to the abos, the aborigines, whose names are all around one in Sydney, in Woolloomooloo, in Parramatta or in Woop Woop, but whose physical presence is but a wisp or a shadow in the thriving city.

Most of the aborigines of these parts were exterminated, by imported disease or by brute force, within a few decades of the first white settlement. Yet two centuries later a few hundred cling to their roots in Sydney, at the very site of the European coming. They are called "coories" here, and like the water of the harbor, like the exotic foliage of the parks and headlands, they are a reminder of stranger, older things than Kev and his kind can conceive. To some Australians the aborigines are a blot on the conscience, to others just a pain in the neck: still, in the end most people thought the coories were worth feeling sorry for, and feel sorry for them I did.

Though their community has produced some celebrities in its time, notably boxers, they live mostly in more luckless quarters of the town, and do not show much as a rule. As it chanced, however, while I was in Sydney this time they celebrated Aboriginal Day. The aboriginal flag of gold, black and yellow flew, to the consternation of Old Australians, side by side with the national flag on Sydney Town Hall, and a march through town was announced, to be followed by a rally at Alexandria Park. Alas, all this went sadly awry. Nobody seemed to know where the march was to begin, or when, somebody pulled the flag down from the Town Hall, not everyone seemed to have mastered the rally chant—*What do we want? Land rights! What have we got? Bugger all!*—and the arrangements ran so late that when the time came for speeches everyone had gone home. "They are a *random* people," was the convincing explanation I was given, when I asked if this was true to coorie form.

By the time I reached Alexandria Park Aboriginal Day seemed to have fizzled out altogether, and all I found was a small huddle of dark-skinned people around an open bonfire, surrounded by litter on the edge of the green. They greeted me with a wan concern, offering me beer out of an ice-bucket, sidling around me rather, and occasionally winking. A small thin boy with cotton wool stuffed in one ear wandered here and there leading a black puppy on a string. Others kicked a football about in the gathering dusk, and around the fire a handful of older men and women looked sadly into the flames. A strong smell of alcohol hung over us, and the man with the bucket urged me quietly, again and again, to have one for the road, dear. Had the rally been a success? I asked. "Yeah," they said, and looked into the fire.

I *did* feel sorry for them. They were like last wasted survivors from some primeval holocaust, whose memories of their own civilization were aeons ago expunged. Did they have a Sydney all their own, I wondered, long ago near the beginnings of time? Did their flag fly braver then? When I said goodbye and drove away ("Go on, dear, just one") the lights of the downtown tower blocks were shining in the distance: but in the shadows at the edge of the park the bonfire flames were dancing still, and the frail figures of the indigenes moved unsteadily in the flicker.

–o / o / o –

One morning I went to Iceland, the skating rink, to watch the Sydney people skating. They did it, as they do most things, very well. Their tall strong frames looked well on the ice. Once more I was struck by the Scandinavian analogy, so Nordic does an Australian look when you put him in cold circumstances, but eventually my attention was gripped by a figure who, it seemed to me, could be nothing else but Aussie.

He was about five years old, blond, lively, tough and unsmiling. He could not, it seemed, actually skate, but he was adept at running about the rink on his blades, and his one purpose of the morning was to gather up the slush that fell off other peoples' boots, and throw it at passing skaters. This task he pursued with skillful and unflagging zeal. Hop,

hop, he would abruptly appear upon the rink, and picking a lively target, staggering his way across the ice, inexorably he would hunt that victim down until *slosh!* the missile was dispatched—and hobble hobble, quick as a flash he was out of the rink again, gathering more material.

I admired him immensely. He hardly ever fell over, he seldom missed, and he did everything with a dexterous assiduity. When I asked him his name he spelt out GORGE with his finger on the rail of the rink; when I asked him if he was enjoying himself he just nodded grimly; and in my mind's eye I saw him thirty years from now, exploding into a company meeting perhaps, with an irresistible take-over, or relentlessly engineering the resignation of a rival under-secretary. I kept my eye firmly on him as I walked out of Iceland, for instinct told me he was assembling slush for me.

Australia was not built by kindness, nor even by idealism. Convicts, not pilgrims, were its Fathers, and Sydney remains rather steelier than it looks. It is not a very sentimental city, and not much given I fear to un-requitable kindness. There is a certain kind of Sydney face, especially among women, which at first sight looks altogether straight, square and reliable, but which examined more carefully (surreptitiously if possible, over the edge of a newspaper from the next table) reveals a latent mean-ness or foxiness inherited surely, I tell myself in my romantic way, from the thuggery of the penal colonies.

Here are a few graffiti I have jotted down in Sydney: CHINKS HIRED, YOU'RE FIRED. WHITE BUT UGLY. THE POLICE KILLED LYOL TITMARCH. NO SCABS OR ASIANS. TURKISH MURDERERS. Behind the pleasant façade of this city, harsher things are always happening. Inexplicable political scandals excite the newspapers. Numberless Royal Commissions investigate improprieties. Through this apparently egalitarian society stalks a handful of gigantic capitalists, with tentacles that seem to extend into every cranny of city life, and make you feel that whatever you are doing, whether you are buying an ice-cream or booking an airline ticket, you are making the same rich Australians richer yet. Immigrants say that your older Ocker is a terrible bigot still, and even now they tell me a foreign accent often gets snubs and indignities—and not only a European accent, for the fa-vorite Sydney witticism of the day is the New Zealand Joke ("How d'you set up a New Zealander in a small business?" "Give him a big one, and wait").

Sydney people strike me as essentially cautious or suspicious in their social attitudes. They lack the gift of spontaneous welcome or generosity. They are too easily embarrassed. Invariably smiling and helpful though this citizenry seems, and quite exceptionally polite, I sometimes think that if I were in real trouble, friendless, destitute and passport-less in the streets, I might feel less abandoned in Manhattan. I considered making the experiment as a matter of fact, and presenting myself on the Circular Quay to beg passers-by for my ferry fare: but I remembered that look in the eye of the ladies at the next table, and lost my nerve.

Even now, two centuries after the event, a streak of bad origins is still apparent in Sydney. Truth will out! It has been smudged in the historical memory—if you can believe the Australians, none of the transported convicts ever did anything worse than poach a squire's salmon, or tumble his daughter in the hay. It has been romanticized, too—in the figure of the larrikin for instance, the Sydney street urchin of ballad and anecdote who used to strut picturesquely about these streets in bell-bottom trousers and pointed shoes, fighting merry gang wars and picking pockets. Today it has been varnished over with layer upon layer of gentility and sophistication, but it is there all the same, and if you want to see it plain, try going to the park on a Sunday afternoon, when the Sydney soap-box orators give vent to their philosophies, and the hecklers to their interruptions. In most countries I love these arenas of free expression—they are rich in picaresque episode and eccentricity, and sometimes even in wisdom. I left Sydney's Speakers' Corner though, with a shudder. The free speech was too grossly free, too crudely spiteful, sexist and foul-mouthed. The arguments were bludgeonly, the humor was coarse, and all around the soap-boxes there strode a horribly purposeful figure, wearing a beret tipped over his eyes, and holding a sheaf of newspaper, whose only purpose was to shout down every speaker in turn, whatever the subject or opinion, with a devastating loutishness of retort—never silent, never still, hurling offensive gibes at speaker and audience alike with a flaming offensive energy.

Now where, said I to myself, have I seen that fellow before? And with a pang I remembered: GORGE the indefatigable ice-slosher, up at the ice-rink.

$-o\,/\,o\,/\,o-$

After lunch one day (Warm Salad, believe it or not, with Chicken Liver) I met Kev in the elevator, with three of his friends from the office. They stood there in silence, sometimes shifting on their feet. "I've just eaten," I ventured for conversation's sake, "a plate of Warm Salad," but it did not make them smile. They looked at me anxiously, trying hard to think of a reply. "Good," managed Kev himself at last, and with relief, murmuring polite and embarrassed excuses, they left me at the 17th floor.

Away to the west of Sydney, over a long innocuous hinterland of suburbs, neither ugly nor beautiful, neither poor nor rich, with Lebanese laundries, and pubs with names like the Gladstone Arms or the Lord Nelson, and ladies in flowered housecoats exercising their dogs at lunchtime, and pizza houses with blown-up pictures of Vesuvius behind their counters, and streets called Myrtle Street and Merryland Road—out there beyond the western suburbs you can see the outline of the Blue Mountains. Snow falls up there sometimes, and log fires burn in resort hotels: and beyond them again, beyond Orange and Dubbo, there begins the almost unimaginable emptiness of Australia, extending mile after mile after mile of scrub, waste and desert into the infinite never-never of the aborigines. Nearly all Australia is empty. Emptiness is part of the Australian state of things, and it reaches out of that wilderness deep into the heart of Sydney itself, giving a hauntingly absent sense to the city, and restraining the responses of advertising executives in elevators.

The scrub is always near. The splodges of green everywhere make this metropolis feel, even now, like an interloper in the wasteland, and people commute daily into Sydney from country that is almost virgin bush. Only just outside the metropolitan-limits, up on the Hawkesbury River, are communities that still cannot be reached by road, to which the mail goes out each day on a chugging river-boat, nosing its way among the creeks and channels, between woodlands where wallabies leap and koalas ruminate, to be unloaded on rickety wharfs at hamlets of shacks and bungalows, and hobbled away with by aged oystermen—the air-conditioned towers of Sydney itself hardly out of sight beyond the gum trees!

The sea everywhere, insidiously entering the city in a myriad inlets, seems a vacuous kind of ocean, which seldom brings the tang of a salt breeze into the downtown streets, and often looks to me indeed like fresh water all the time. The history of Sydney, like the history of Australia, is essentially blank, very little of interest ever having happened here, and there is a sort of bloodlessness even to the very success of the place, and a pallor to its style, and a curious suggestion of muffle even at rush-hour, which reminds one repeatedly of that immense desolation beyond the hills.

This sensation preoccupies many Australian artists, and affects me very strangely. Sometimes in Sydney I feel I am not looking directly at the city at all, but seeing it through glass, or perhaps reflected in a mirror. Its edges seem oddly ill-defined when I am in such a mood, its pellucid light is lacking in refraction, without the opacity of dust, breath, history and regret that hangs on the air of most great cities. The wind seems to have been filtered through some pale mesh of the south. Even the seafood, however imaginatively garnished with strawberries or avocado, seems to lack the tang of the deep sea and the tides. Even the Australian language sometimes sounds to me echo-like, as though it is reaching me from far, far away, or out of another time.

Sydney can be exhilarating, but it is a *moderate* exhilaration. It can stir the heart, but not quite to the point of ecstasy. You do not dance along these streets, or thrill to the beat of the place. Its faces, in repose, are neither kind nor cruel, but just expressionless. People seldom seem surprised in Sydney, and for that matter they are seldom very surprising themselves: though it is astonishing that so grand a place should exist down here at all, so handsome, so complete a metropolis on the edge of nowhere, still it never gives the impression, as other young civic prodigies do, that it has burst irresistibly out of the sub-soil into life.

Here are two old Hungarians walking on a Sydney beach. They wear hats, camel coats and signet rings. They came here half a lifetime ago out of the shambles of Europe, and they have lived happily ever after. They escaped the murder of war and the miseries of Communism to prosper in this peaceful haven of the Antipodes. Their wives are taking coffee at the Cosmopolitan—remember the two in furs, silent over their Camparis? Their sons, daughters and grandchildren are probably out in their boats. They are very lucky, and know it. "We are very lucky," they say. "Sydney is a beautiful city. Australia is the Best Country in the World." They do not say it *con amore,* though, or even *cantabile.* They seem unlikely to kiss the soil they walk on, or raise their hands in gratitude to the Australian dream. "Let us hope the world stays in peace," they simply conclude, as if to say, let's hope our luck lasts out—just give us ten more years, O God of the Southern Sun!

Most people like Australia, but in this city of the numbed reflex, the blank eye, few will open their hearts about the place: just as Kev and his colleagues in the elevator, I feel sure, must have bottled up some frightfully witty retorts about the Warm Salad.

– o / o / o –

Far up the coasts of Sydney, north and south of the Sydney Heads that form the spectacular portal of Australia, comfortable villas of the well-to-do lie encouched in fig trees, gums and lawns of buffalo grass. They are seldom ostentatious houses. They are not like the garden palaces of Cap d'Antibes, or the monastically enclosed pads of Hollywood. Though it is true that the Sydney *jeunesse dorée* is given to things like flying by sea-plane to take lunch in suburban restaurants, or giving birthday parties for favorite Ferraris, still history, temperament and politics have combined to ensure that this is not a city of conspicuous consumption. Its extremely rich are seldom visible, if only because they are in Europe or California; and its glossiest mansions cannot be seen either, because they are country houses set in 25,000 acres of sheep country somewhere over the hills. All this gives the city an air of calm stability: the very idea of economic collapse, still less revolution, seems preposterous, as I look out of my hotel window now to see the white yachts at play in the harbor, yet another laughing horde of schoolchildren storming the terraces of the Opera House, and Kev at his window in his shirt-sleeves, preparing himself psychologically for the long jog home.

Short of another world catastrophe, I think, this place has reached its fulfillment. This is it. It will probably get richer, it will certainly get more Asian, but aesthetically, metaphysically, my bones tell me I am already seeing the definitive Sydney, the more or less absolute Australia. A few more tower blocks here, an extra suburb there, a louder Chinatown, more futuristic ferry-boats perhaps—otherwise, this is how Sydney is always going to be. That bland pallor of personality will survive, that seen-through-a-glass quality, and visitors from the north will always be able to fancy, as they look out at the harbor's odd foliage and wide skies, that they have been deposited upside-down on the obverse of the world. The strain of shyness, the old streak of the brutal, will be held in balance still: another zealot will always be collecting slush at the ice-rink, another generation of satisfied entrepreneurs will ask destiny for just another decade of happiness, just long enough to live out their lives in the Best Country in the World.

I have been at pains to draw the warts of Sydney in, but on the whole, I have to say, few cities on earth have arrived at so agreeable a fulfillment. Those old Hungarians are right—they are very lucky people, whose fates have washed them up upon this brave and generally decent shore. But just as no man is a hero to his valet, so no city is a paragon to its inhabitants, especially at the end of a hard day in the office, and by 5.30 Kev's morning euphoria has long worn off. The ferries down there are jammed to the gunwales with commuters. The bridge looks solid with traffic. It is drizzling again. Bugger it, Kev remembers, tonight's the night for Andrew and Marge—avocados again, you can bet your life, and they'll probably bring that snotty brat Dominic to crawl around the table. "Night, Mr. Evans." Night Avrie, silly cow. "Night Kev." Night Jim, you potbellied Ocker. "Just before you go, Kev, heard this one? There's this New Zealander. . . ."

Jeez this rain is miserable. Get out of the road, you silly sod. Christ, who dreamed up that Opera House? (We all know who paid for it, don't we.) Avocado and prawns, you can bet your life. What was that woman on about in the elevator? Warm Salad! Shit! Look at that traffic! Look at that madman in the Fairmont! Who'd live in a town like this, I ask you. Warm Salad! We must all be bloody loonies. . . .

"Kev! Kev, is that you? Marge and Andrew are here, dear, and they've brought little Dominic with them."

Fun City

LAS VEGAS, U.S.A.

It was the Piazza San Marco in Venice that first entered my mind when I strolled down from my bedroom ("A Steady Red Light Reminds You That You Have Requested A Special Service") into the casino of the MGM Grand Hotel in Las Vegas. There was no sunshine in the great room, of course, which was plunged into a timeless twilight, no sparkle of old mosaic or streaked alabaster: but what took me instantly back to Venice was the music.

On one side of the room, near the booking-office for scenic flights to the Grand Canyon, a pianist named Jerry Brown was playing *Georgia on My Mind*. On the other side, half-hidden in the gloom of the bar, Sasha Semenoff and his Romantic Strings were playing *One Enchanted Evening*. The two strains clashed somewhere in the middle, above the blackjack tables, and with their jumble of beat and style, their blend of the wistful and the ebullient, their cheerful discord and their unflagging energy, they reminded me at once of that other, older pleasure-dome far away, where the café orchestras of Quadri's and Florian's strum away in competition through the summer evenings.

And there was no denying the sense of pleasure to the MGM casino that day. The crowds that poured ceaselessly through its front doors, past the stone naiads spouting water through their nipples, fairly shone with excited anticipation. Beside Mr. Brown's piano a little crowd of southern folk, arm in arm in check shirts, was swaying sentimentally to the beat of the music, while in the bar a rather grander group in evening dress sat in a condition of frozen but distinctly flattered embarrassment as Mr. Semenoff and his Strings played *Rosemarie* very close to their ears, Mr. Semenoff smiling graciously throughout while the more winsome of his lady violinists swooped here and there to the line of the melody, throwing pretty laughs over her shoulder.

I can see her now! And beyond her, a jumbled shifting picture of the huge casino floor, the pools of its lights on the green felt of the gambling-tables, the gesticulating beefy figures throwing crap, the ladderman high on his chair above the baccarat players, the ceaseless movement of the dealers' hands, the slow watchful patrol of the floor-walkers and pit-bosses, the long, long line of holiday-makers being ushered by security men, guns at their hips, towards their evening with Mr. Englebert Humperdink in the Celebrity Room (itself sealed like a lush bordello beside the cashiers' cages)—and all around, dimly glowing, the crowded ranks of the fruit machines, clanking, winking sometimes, attended by dim crouched figures holding paper cups, and now and then erupting into a shrill ringing of bells, a clatter of jackpot coins and raucous shrieks of triumph.

Even as I arrived a middle-aged lady, wearing blue slacks that sagged slightly around her buttocks, and a straw hat with uncut edges such as Huck Finn liked to sport, detached herself from these mechanisms and suddenly burst into a solitary but exuberant jitter-bug, clicking her thumbs and waving her forefinger in the half-light. The southerners around the piano whistled and clapped. Mr. Brown deftly adjusted his rhythms. "Well" I said to myself as I passed gingerly by, "this may not be so bad. It's hardly Venice after all, but it looks more fun than Gomorrah."

–o / o / o–

"Have your fun, Jan," said the Leading Citizen, "sure thing, this is a Fun Town, but what we specially do not like is these comparisons with Sodom and such. What people forget is that here in Vegas we have a thriving civic-minded community. We have 130 church buildings, Jan, in this city of ours. We have a thriving university, Jan. We are rapidly becoming the cultural center of the desert Southwest. I think I could safely say that you won't find a more lovely home environment anywhere than some of our high-grade home environments here. Mr. Wayne Newton the famous singer breeds his Arab horses in our city. Mr. Liberace is another of our distinguished residents. What I want you to remember, Jan, is this—the Spanish Trail came this way, right over this very spot, before the game of roulette ever entered the Infant Republic—that's what I always tell people like you, who come inquiring—before the game of roulette ever entered the Infant Republic of the United States!"

And it is true that around the perimeters of Las Vegas, where the ever-growing city extends raggedly into the desert, a middle-sized western railway center strives to honor family values and civilized norms. Street after street the homes of the Vegas bourgeoisie extend in wholesome conformity, and the people who hose their cars on the sidewalks, or bathe in the perpetual summer sunshine on their sprinkled lawns, have that slightly cheesy, well-meaning look indigenous to all the American West, and compounded I think of climate, religion, Swedish grandmothers and rather too much ice-cream.

Mormons actually founded Las Vegas, only its name (which means "The Meadows") being left from the overnighters of the Spanish Trail, and its original reputation was nothing if not devout. The Saints ran a mission station here, and though they were still in their polygamous phase they were certainly no Babylonians. To this day they are powerful in Las Vegas banking and commerce; the place was born again in quite another sense in 1905 when the railway town was established, and yet again in 1931 when gambling was legalized in Nevada, but still their astute rectitude seems to set the tone for Vegas suburban life.

A trace of sanctimony is inescapable among this citizenry. When a few years ago the electorate was asked whether "adult-oriented theatres and bookstores" should be allowed in the city, a three-to-one majority said no. After I left the Leading Citizen I called, at his suggestion, upon Christian Supplies, one of the best-known commercial enterprises in town. It is a very cornucopia of spiritual riches, and through it all day long Las Vegans browse for holy comics, uplifting license plates, Jesus patches or Born Again literature ("Every Tract a Proven Soulwinner"). Mrs. Shine runs the place, and I asked her which version of the Holy Bible Las Vegas Christians chiefly bought, surmising (I blush to say) that they might prefer some Inspirational Paraphrase. She answered me rather sternly. The King James Authorized version, she said, of 1611.

There is inevitably a trace of the comic to these yearnings, Las Vegas being notoriously what it is—the very face of the good lady at the airport information desk, doling out church directories, speaks to us all inescapably of humbug. But it is not all hypocrisy. Las Vegas really does contain a decent enough western town within itself, struggling if not to get out, at least to reveal or fulfill itself. There are many families here in the truest pioneer tradition, like the Cashmans who now run the Cadillac agency but whose progenitor Big Jim Cashman began by running a sandwich shop for the railroad construction workers, or the Mikulichs who now own the Vegas-Reno buses but came to the town from Yugoslavia in 1913.

You can hear good music nowadays in Vegas, if you pop up to the Artemus W. Ham Concert Hall. You can go to a straight play or a classical ballet, at the university. There is a Jewish community paper, the *Las Vegas Israelite,* which is full of Mothers of the Year and congratulations to Eli Welt on his election to the Board of Directors of the Nevada Retail Association: there is a bright young magazine called the *Las Vegan* which reports its proper share of Bubbles and Baubles fetes, lovely home environments and country club poolside barbecues.

The proprietors of the *Las Vegan,* as a matter of fact, threw a little party for me, and the people I met there were certainly not *all* humbugs. There was a novelist, and a well-known photographer, and a couple of academics, and a designer with an Australian wife, and a number of intelligent girls who said I *couldn't* write about Vegas until I had seen the Spring Mountains or the Red Rock Canyon. Agreeable infants kept burbling in and out filching canapés, and there was African folk-art on the walls.

One of my fellow guests ran an art gallery in town, and as we parted she gave me an envelope containing, she said, a little souvenir of my visit. When I opened it I found inside a photograph of a work by her father, a famous Italo-American sculptor. It showed a naked girl of total innocence sleeping side by side with an adorable little fawn, and it was called "The Dream."

"Kinky postcards, huh?" said a man looking over my shoulder.

—o / o / o—

There is always a sneer in Las Vegas. The mountains around it sneer. The desert sneers. And arrogant in the middle of its wide valley, dominating those diligent sprawling suburbs, the downtown city sneers like anything.

There is no other city center like this. Even in the early 1950s, when I first came to Las Vegas, the shape of the place was detectably Western Traditional, clustered around the railway depot and the city hall—overlaid even then indeed by the gaudy stamp of the casinos, but still recognizably a halt on the line of the Union Pacific. Today only the railroad tracks themselves delineate the past. All else is Fun City. The depot itself is actually absorbed into a casino block, so that you can step from the train direct into a gambling hall, while the downtown streets are unrecognizable as any kind of ordinary town center, the drug stores and hardware merchants, if there are any, being altogether overwhelmed in neonry and hucksterism.

Out of the old Freemont and 5th Street crossing, where Ferron's Drugs used to be, has been unleashed the blazing esplanade called the Strip, only thinly disguised as Las Vegas Boulevard South—four miles long, intermittently speckled with gigantic resort hotels, and filled in everywhere else with clubs, wedding chapels, motels with complimentary blue movies and mirror-ceilings, car rentals, Le Petit Mozart French Restaurant and Bogie's the male strip-joint (defined by its general manager recently as being "not a pornographic-type situation").

It is as though some inconceivable alien organism has fallen upon the old depot town, squatting there athwart the tracks and infecting everything with some incurable, unidentifiable but not altogether disagreeable virus. Nobody in Vegas can escape the emanations of this incubus. Even Mrs. Shine, after long wrestlings with her conscience, steels herself to pass between the gambling tables now and then to indulge herself in a buffet luncheon on the Strip. Even Pastor Harry Ward is ready sometimes to leave his Fellowship Center (Sunday School 1 p.m.) to officiate at the Chapel of the Roses round the corner, where an instant candlelight wedding with piped-in music need cost no more than 30 bucks, Amex cards accepted.

Almost nobody is immune. The Leading Citizen himself allows that gambling and whoring have always been, after all, an essential factor in the western *mores,* and Mr. Parry Thomas, the Mormon chairman of the Valley Bank, was the very first banker to put his money behind the gaming industry. Nearly every Vegas supermarket has its own fruit machines; a stone's throw away from Christian Supplies stands the Gamblers' Bookstore, the biggest gambling bookshop on earth, where the dedicated punter may buy anything from Dr. Robert Lewis's *Taking Chances: The Psychology of Losing* to Mr. Charles Cotton's *The Compleat Gambler,* which he published in 1674, only 63 years after the Authorized Version.

This is Fun City—and as I surmised that first day, some of it *is* fun. There is the fun of gambling itself, to which I am by no means impervious. There is the somewhat blowzy fun of Showbiz, the Stars, the Hollywood Spectaculars, Sammy Davis, Jr., and all that. There is the undeniable fun of the hundreds of thousands of neon lights that emblazon the presence of Las Vegas so astonishingly upon the night. There is the fun of the ever-shifting parade of visitors—twelve million of them last year, or some 48 times the resident population.

You must be a purist indeed not to get some fun from the tomfool architecture of Las Vegas, with its monstrous classic motifs, the gigantic heroic statuary of Caesar's Palace, those breast-gushing nymphs of the MGM, and its megalomaniac suggestions of wealth, power and grandeur. The sheer loudness and brassiness of Las Vegas is entertaining, and there is a true beauty, too, to the sight of the city flashing and winking away there, a restless cauldron of lights, seen from the surrounding hills in the middle of the night—all alone in the desert, an inconceivable oasis, with the headlights streaming into town from the Los Angeles highway, and the landing lights of the jets coming and going from McCarran International.

It reaches some kind of apogee in the resort called Circus Circus, which is housed in a gigantic mock-marquee, and offers free circus acts every half-hour noon until midnight from here to eternity. This is a kind of Piranesi Big Top, a labyrinth of alcoves, ramps, roundabouts, staircases, stalls and arcades, so mysteriously constructed, so dazzling with massed battalions of fruit machines, so loud with the clanging of handles and the booming of loudspeaker voices, so rushed about by candy-floss goblins, that for myself I wander through it altogether bemused. Ever and again I seem to pass the booth where children are made up to look like clowns— at every turn I encounter that stall of grotesquely swollen teddy-bears and pink Plutos—before every fruit machine the same fat white lady goggles— at every table seems to sit the self-same dealer, in pink shirt and gypsy sleeves, bald as a coot and largely labelled "Curly"—round and round for ever on revolving carousels the same solemn couples suck at their thick pink drinks beneath the transcendental lights.

When I first looked in at Circus Circus the Paulo Sisters were in the middle of their trapeze act. Their father was watching them from the side of the ring, and he told me that they were half German and half English, and had spent all their lives on the professional circuit, living in trailers. At that moment they were reaching the climax of their performance, when one sister, sustaining the other by her teeth, flips her into the Helicopter Spin and whirls her upside-down at 60 miles an hour above the ring.

It seemed to me that this must be one of life's most muddling experiences. Circus Circus is disorienting enough as it is: think how disturbing it must all look, the pink plastic dogs, the thick sweet drinks, the flashing lights, Curly and all the fat white gamblers, seen the wrong way up at a mile a minute! But the Paulo Sisters concluded their act with composure, and curtseying gracefully to the crowd, danced away off-stage without a sign of vertigo. Dad collected the props together for the next time round.

– o / o / o –

The fat white woman that nobody loves is the truest familiar of Las Vegas, pulling her handle mindlessly any hour of day or night, in the roughest downtown betting parlor as in the poshest casinos of the Strip. Mention this city to travellers anywhere, and it is she they will most vividly recall—not the flashy big spenders, not the Hollywood personalities of the showrooms, not the visiting sheikhs or Japanese, certainly not the Prominent Citizen, but that tranced soul at the fruit machine, clutching her paper cup like a bowl of sacrament.

For myself it is her fatness I chiefly notice. Las Vegas is the world capital of obesity. You can buy chocolate by the yard or the bucket at the Candy Jar in town, and there are more fat people here at any one time than there are Muslims in Mecca. When each group of merry-makers enters the Circus Circus, they literally burst into view, gigantic buttocks and immeasurable thighs, paunches bulging over trouser tops, dilated white arms and bosoms like gas balloons. It is like a Hall of Mirrors, and as they lumber away into the twilight assiduously licking their ice-creams, I almost expect them to be elongated into skinny giants, or squashed into flat folk.

The Man Who Broke the Bank at Monte Carlo would not feel at home in Vegas—this is no town for a gentleman. It is the Xanadu of the second-rate. It even made me feel a bit of a snob, so coarse is the style of it, so unfastidious: according to Mr. Ralph Pearl, the chronicler of Las Vegas life, when Jacqueline Kennedy once made the mistake of coming here the check-room lady at the Dunes described her afterwards as "a broad who peed icicles"—a fitting Las Vegan epithet for disdain. I shudder to think of the dirty stories that are told in this city every night: I squirm to remember the effigies of President Carter on sale in the MGM Grand itself, with an erect cactus for his penis; I am embarrassed despite myself, for I am honestly no prude, to pick up the *Las Vegas Mirror* and find within it advertisements for Whips, Clamps and Doc Johnson's Pet Jock, "for the woman who deserves more."

It is a Xanadu of the middle-aged, too. Young American, it seems, does not generally take to gambling, and the Vegas pilgrims are likely to have learnt to throw crap in the army, or even in the Depression. The behemoth Cadillacs that are still the thing in Vegas perfectly suit their visions of fulfillment, and the aging entertainers who are super-stars of the Strip perfectly suit their tastes—Eddie Fisher, Tom Jones, Dean Martin, Liberace himself. The MGM Grand is decorated with photographs of Spencer Tracy, Clark Gable *et al.,* and its house cinema perpetually screens such nostalgic oldies as *Gone with the Wind* or *Mutiny on the Bounty:* when I squinted through my door-hole one evening I saw framed in the corridor outside an ancient pair of lovers, grey and scrawny, locked in a lascivious embrace whose very pose (she with one leg cocked behind her, he in blue suspenders) spoke to me direct from the 1940s.

They still have Happy Hours in the Las Vegas resorts. You still hear phrases like "You betcha" and "Looky here" at its bars. Gossip columns of ghastly sycophancy ornament the local papers, and Mr. Dick Maurice's nightly chat-show on local TV ("Success Speaks for Itself!") is absolutely the worst of its kind I have ever seen anywhere in the world. Every aspect of the American fraud is accentuated in Las Vegas, in rubbery victuals and false bonhomie, in meaningless greeting and programmed response. "Well, hi, howya doin'?" say the waitresses in their sincerity voices, "ready for sump'n to putya on top of the world? Howzabout our Pecan-and-Broiled-Lobster-Tail Pizza?": and when one day, just as an experiment, I rang the Secret Witness line, upon which you may give confidential evidence to the police, exactly the same voice answered me, with just the same computer brightness.

Nor is the sin of Las Vegas, the point of it all, free, frank and lusty in the western tradition. Prostitution, for instance, is legal elsewhere in Nevada, and famous bordellos like the Chicken Ranch and the Cherry Patch flourish mightily. In Las Vegas itself they are still forbidden, and so the squalid old profession is made more squalid still with pimpery and imprisonment, with patrolling plainclothes cops and 40 percent pay-offs to hotel concierges. Most of the tourists would be horrified to be seen in their Vegas circumstances, when they go home to Spring Vale or Okokie— Mrs. Hooper of the Friday coffee-meetings ogling the strippers at Bogie's, Jim from the First City Bank out on the town with the boys, picking up a tart or two like they used to over in Europe, or rolling the dice with the injunctions of his boyhood—"That's the way baby, roll it my way hon!"— as they did at Spring High long ago.

Sometimes, early in the morning, I went for a brisk walk along the Strip before the sun burst over the mountain and clamped all Vegas within its air-conditioning. This was a dispiriting experience. Just before dawn is the only moment when Vegas, just for an hour or so, abandons its pretenses. The civic make-up is distinctly worn, in that brief limbo-time; even the sincerity-smiles are dimmed. Some of the neon lights are still flashing, some are dark already, and through the open doors of the casinos you may see exhausted gamblers slumped over their coffees, or wan svelte figures in tuxedos and jewelled dresses sitting like mummies, dead already, around their ghostly baccarat.

Once or twice on these dawn forays I met joggers, incongruously sweating along the Strip, but more often, through the empty quiet, figures of the night before appeared: pale hookers on their sidewalks still, unshaven glassy revellers, taxi-loads of chorus girls going home to bed, dealers with red eyes, ash-heavy cigarettes and jackets slung over their shoulders climbing heavily into their cars. There was nothing very stimulating to this scene. It was not like the dawn hour in a really great city, when life itself seems to be changing gear around you, in the unfailing excitement of a new day. In Vegas the excitement is all contrived. Truly exciting things seldom happen here, and dawn is the time of the Vegan truth, when even the Fun flags.

−o / o / o −

On and on the fat white women wander, perfect Vegas-fodder, putting the money in, pulling the handle, and occasionally breaking away to dance alone beside the piano. And nobody, I soon discovered, was better material for Fun City than I was myself. Even at my snootiest I responded like Pavlov's dog to the conditioning of the place. Whatever I do

in Las Vegas, I told myself on my first day there, I will *never* be seen
clutching one of those horrible little paper cups at the fruit machines: but
lo, on the very next day I caught myself before the Silverbird machines
with a cup in my hand as to the manner born, clutching my complimentary Fun Book.

You have to be smarter than me to resist Dr. Pavlov in Las Vegas, for
nothing is guileless here. Even the very rich, whom you may see arriving
at the airport in their chartered junket flights, to be met by obsequious
Cadillacs and swept away to complimentary penthouses—even the fa-
vored guests of the management, who are known in the trade as "comps,"
are as absolutely Vegas-fodder as the rest of us: the odds are stacked just
as heavily against them, the attitude of their hosts, if rather smarmier, is
just as calculating. Nothing is spontaneous in Vegas, and little is what it
seems. It has all been counted beforehand, and through the one-way mirrors and hidden screens of the casinos careful eyes are watching all the
time. ("Casino supervisors," darkly observes *Rouge et Noir,* the trade
newsletter, "are instructed to note any significant cash action and identi-
fying information of individuals displaying significant action.")

Las Vegas is a very clever place. It is a magnet to specialists and craftsmen of a hundred kinds, who live out there in the suburbs with Mrs.
Shine and the Prominent Citizen, but who come to work each day (or
each night) in the eye of the neon hurricane. They range from the electronic experts to service the fruit machines (themselves, with micro-
processing, getting cleverer all the time) to the hotel landscape gardeners,
the display-lighting engineers, or the professional players of Jai Alai imported specially from the Basque country for demonstration games at the
MGM Grand.

It is a town, for instance, of innumerable musicians. They have come
here from all over the world, they make a secure and comfortable living
in the café orchestras and showbands, and off-duty they often combine
for symphonic and chamber music, or play jazz for their own amuse-
ment. Take Mr. Semenoff of the Romantic Strings. He is a Latvian Jew
by birth, and emerged from wartime concentration camps to study the
violin in Munich. He came to Vegas twenty years ago, and now leads his
delightful ensemble every evening at the MGM, when you can always
find him, between performances, snatching a coffee with his violin beside
him for all the world as though he were playing at the old Gellert in Budapest, say, or one of the posher cafés on the Vienna Ringstrasse.

Dancers abound here too, and designers, and animal-trainers, and cho-
reographers, and magicians—"there's generally a magician or two in
here," they told me at the Gamblers' Bookstore, looking around in vain
for wizardly looking persons, "but they seem to have vanished just now."
And the most dedicated specialists of all are the casino men themselves,
the general staff of this motley army. They seemed to me a joyless kind
of people. The ones I met seldom smoked, drank sparely, never gambled,
were slow to grasp the meaning of a joke and viewed the surrounding
phantasmagora with a hard, analytical, absolutely dispassionate eye. The
Vegan machine is very finely tuned, and casino men are not all the dark-
jowled thugs of popular legend. Mr. Bill Friedman of the Castaways, for
example, is an internationally known authority on the theory and history
of gambling, and many another keen brain is at work behind these showy
scenes, assessing the future in penthouse offices, observing the trends over
the luncheon tables of the Las Vegas Country Club.

Most of Las Vegas's gamblers, of course, rich and poor, are pure suck-
ers. They know they are: they are treating themselves, just for a day or
two, to what the poet Coleridge defined in quite another context as "the
willing suspension of disbelief." Not a trick is lost to milch them, from
the fruit machines so inescapably disposed to the rock-bottom restaurant
prices, genuinely cheaper than Mom can do it, that broke the resistance of
Mrs. Shine (I did not myself succumb to the Circus Circus offer of a 29-
cent Biscuit and Gravy Breakfast, but I did try the Four Queens $1
shrimp cocktail, of which they claim to have sold *ten million*). The look
in the corporate eye of the Strip is a very cold and steady look, and its
spokesmen have a habit of letting you talk your silly head off before offering any hint of a reply, a technique unnervingly reminiscent, I thought,
of Lubianka.

For the Vegan cynicism at its most debased, try the wedding chapels.
There are scores of them along the Strip, and with every permutation of
sickly sentiment they offer immediate ecstasy to several thousand lovers
every month. Everything is taken care of. Will you be requiring Honeymoon Garters, Just Married T-Shirts, Bumper Stickers, Everlasting Roses—
flowers are, after all, Love's Truest Language? Will a video-tape of the
ceremony be needed? Witnesses can be arranged, naturally, and recorded
bells can be chimed, if required, after the Reverend's matrimonial address.

I slipped into a wedding chapel one afternoon, between marriages, and
tried to imagine how it would be to dedicate one's future life before

the Reverend there. It was hardly a silent meditation. A rattle of air-conditioning disturbed it, and somewhere out of sight behind the artificial mahogany panelling I could hear the chapel receptionist engaged in a protracted gossip on the telephone (tantalizing gossip, too—"say, I got to see him," I heard her say, "he got married and I got to ride off with him, she was in the other car . . ."). Never mind, the Authorized Version was opened on its lectern at the Book of Proverbs, and the plastic puttis upholding the ceiling looked down at me sweetly, through their ribbons and forget-me-not posies, over the pink-bound copy of *Love Story* which each pair of them was holding.

I sat there for a moment and thought about it all, and narrowed the focus of matrimony's grand conception to this shoddy little shack of legerdemain opposite the motel check-in. I tried to hear the noble words of the great commitment spouted up there by the Reverend for his 10-buck share of the profits. I thought of love itself, the splendor of procreation, too, reduced to the thin strains of the recorded electric organ, and the Honeymoon Garter in its plastic envelope. And just for a moment—my only sententious moment, I hope, during my visit to Las Vegas—I raged within myself: to think that all this was done by choice, by people of grand heritage, born to splendor: to think that those simpering cherubs were surrogates for Michelangelo's celestial angels, or that those vibrato melodies of Togetherness stood in the line of the mighty Bach himself!

–o / o / o–

I shook myself out of it, but anyway the fun had faded by then—and Fun, you will have noticed, is the theme word of this essay as of its subject. Fun City is no fun really, after a day or two, and when the Vegas operators speak of fun, they are using double-speak. The days when the Mafia ran Vegas were Fun Days—the Good Old Days of criminals like Bugsie Malone and Moe Sedway, the "legendary characters" of Vegas, the "old guys." In the garden of the Flamingo Hotel, now a Hilton, an inscription facetiously suggests that its roses may flourish so brightly because Bugsie buried his missing victims there: but there is nothing funny really to the hidden meanings of Las Vegas, its brutal subsoil and its often sinister compost.

Sinister? The adept manipulations of brilliant businessmen? The enterprising vulgarities of Circus Circus? The tinsel of the wedding chapels? Swinging Suzy's, which features Black, English and other Exotic

Escorts? Ah, but there is to the very presence of Las Vegas, I came to feel by the end of my stay, a suggestion of true evil. This is more than a discreet city, where photography is not encouraged and anonymity is respected: it is a profoundly secret one. The myriad security men who prowl it with their guns and dogs properly represent its ruling spirit, and brooding always over it, too, is the knowledge of the nuclear explosions whose mushroom clouds rose above the Vegas horizon not so long ago, of the great Nellis Air Force base whose fighters still do their death-sweeps on its sky, of the missile-pits that lie out there in the desert waiting for Armageddon. It is a place of secrets—if I had to choose one architectural symbol to stand for Las Vegas it would not be some flashy porte-cochère or casino fantasy, but a bare enclave wall of grey concrete, such as surrounds so many of this city's lovelier home environments.

And if I had to choose an emblematic resident, it would be Howard Hughes. He lived in Las Vegas for years, immured in the ninth floor of his own Desert Inn, and at one time owned a large proportion of the Vegas resorts, besides succeeding Vera Krupp, heiress to the German munitions fortune, as proprietor of the old Wilson Ranch. Hughes's arrival on the scene is often credited with the decline of the mobsters in Las Vegas, but his legacy is not all benign. The legends of his endless conspiracies, his association with the CIA, his eerie lifestyle and his tragic destiny haunt the place with a baleful fascination, and perhaps affect its manner to this day. Coups and conspiracies in the Hughes *genre* are endemic to Las Vegas: prominent in the local news when I was there was the financier James Ray Houston, the Silver King, who was said to be minting coins for use in the rebellious island of Santo Spirito in the New Hebrides, besides running a money-laundering based upon entirely fictitious direct communication with a computer in Switzerland. I spent a day wandering around Las Vegas with one of its better-informed newspapermen, and it was instructive how often he pointed out the homes of rich recluses, from Orson Welles whom nobody seems to see to the financier who actually lives underground, with buried swimming-pool and subterranean tennis-court.

The sense of withdrawal is essential to the Vegan ambience, just as the business arrangements of this town are still shrouded in rumor and insinuation. Run through the management lists of the Las Vegas institutions—you will find them in the Chamber of Commerce's VIP List—and any criminologist will identify the unsavory names for you. There are bad men about. Sixty people were murdered in Las Vegas last year. While I was there a woman said she had been told she would be found in the desert with her legs cut off behind the knees if she refused to work as a whore. Before I arrived a citizen was killed by nineteen shots from plainclothes policemen when he stopped at a pizza bar to talk to Anthony Spilotro, better known as Tony the Ant. When they talk nostalgically about the good old days of the hit men, they are only putting to the backs of their minds the ugly truths of today—the willing suspension of disbelief come home ironically to roost! Las Vegas sometimes reminds me of the terrible little towns of inner Sicily or Sardinia, where half the population consists of murderers, kidnappers or extortionists, and the other half pretends not to notice.

The longer I stayed there, the more I was oppressed by this sense of the unthinkable, and in the end I took the advice of that girl in the party, and drove out one brilliant morning through the innocuous suburbs to the Spring Mountains, where the snow still lay pristine above the treeline, and the air was cool and clear. The Las Vegas valley was far out of sight over the mountain ridge, but even so I could not escape the sensations of it: for through the scent of the pines and the morning wind, gradually I became conscious of another smell that I had brought along with me. It clung to me whatever I did, and it was the smell of the Strip: compounded, I think, of air-conditioning, and aerosol fresheners, and deodorants, and a trace of cigar smoke, and paper money, and chewing-gum, and something rotten or acrid which I cannot place exactly, but which I suspect to be the smell of Fun.

A Visit to Barchester

WELLS, ENGLAND

Searching on a wistful whim for Barchester, I came to Wells in Somerset. I craved the Trollopian scene not for itself exactly, but for its myth of a Golden Age. Of course I wanted the incidentals too, the bells across the close, the fine old ladies taking tea beneath college rowing groups featuring, at stroke, their uncle the late Precentor. I wanted the mingled smell of dry rot and market cabbage. I hoped to catch a glimpse of the Organist and Choirmaster, pulling his gown over his shoulders as he hurried across to evensong. But like many other romantics, all over the Western world, I hungered really for the hierarchal certainty of the old England, that amalgam of faith, diligence, loyalty, independence and authority which Trollope mischievously enshrined in the legends of his little city.

At least Wells looks impeccably the part. As one descends from the spooky heights of Mendip, haunted by speleologists and Roman snails, it lies there in the lee of the hills infinitely snug and wholesome. No motorway thunders anywhere near. It is fourteen miles to the nearest railway station. Though Wells has been a city since the tenth century, it is still hardly more than an ample village, dutifully assembled around the towers of the cathedral: and though beyond it one may see the arcane bumps and declivities of the Glastonbury plain, there is nothing very mystical to one's first impression of the place. Its accent is homely Somerset, and its aspect rubicund.

In no time at all I had found myself a room, low-beamed and flower-patterned, in the Crown Hotel overlooking the Market Square, where a rivulet swims limpidly down the gutter past the old town conduit: and hardly less promptly, as it happened, I found myself fined £2 for parking too long outside Penniless Porch, through whose squinted archway the great grey mass of the cathedral itself looked benignly down upon warden and miscreant alike.

$$-o/o/o-$$

Almost at once, too, I met the Dean, actually in the shadow of the Porch. Eton, Oxford and the Welsh Guards, he was not hard to identify. In the cathedral, I later discovered, they call him "Father Mitchell," a disconcerting usage to one of my purposes, but I certainly could not complain about his authenticity *qua* Dean. With a splendid concern his voice rang out, as we sat there on the beggars' bench watching the citizenry pass by. "Good morning, good morning! Lovely day! What a success yesterday— what *would* we have done without you? Morning Simon! Morning Bert! Morning John! (*John Harvey, you know, our greatest authority on medieval church architecture* . . .)"

The Dean of Wells is a very busy man indeed. He showed me his diary, and it was chock-a-block—even Thursday, resolutely marked as his day off, was nibbled into by a meeting of the Judge's Lodgings Committee. It seemed more the life of an impresario than a cleric, and this is because a cathedral nowadays is far more than just a shrine, but is partly a social center, partly a concert hall, partly a tourist attraction, and in the case of Wells, very largely a National Concern. A few years ago it was realized that the west front of Wells Cathedral, incorporating an unrivalled gallery of not very exciting but undeniably medieval statuary, was crumbling away: the consequent appeal, launched by an urbane firm of professional appealers, suddenly made Wells, like Venice, better-known for its decay than for its survival, and added a new dimension to the life of the Very Reverend the Dean.

It crossed my mind, indeed, so ubiquitous were the symptoms of restoration, that the cathedral's chief function had become its own repair. The building itself, clouded with scaffolding, tap-taps with the hammers of the masons. One frequently sees the Dean, cassocked and umbrella'd, gazing with solicitous eyes at a leprous evangelist or precarious cornice. Outside the west doors there stands a superannuated Victorian pillarbox, painted bright blue, for the acceptance of contributions, and hardly a week seems to pass without some fund-raising function beneath the bold inverted arches of the nave (themselves a restorative device, for they were hastily erected when, in 1338, the central tower lurched twelve feet out of true).

But no, the Dean reassured me over lunch, the true focus of cathedral life remained the daily services which, however infinitesimal the congregations, are held now as always in the panelled seclusion of the choir. Behind the scenes the immemorial functions of the cathedral continue, each with its titular chief: the Baron of the Exchequer, the Chancellor, the Master of the Fabric, the Communar, the Chief Steward. The Dean still presides over the Quinque Personae of his Chapter. The Priest-Vicars, the Lay-Vicars, the Canons Residentiary, the vergers, the twenty-one choristers, all are there to offer their gifts and energies to the daily affirmation of the faith.

I took him at his word, and went that afternoon to evensong: or rather, like nearly everybody else in sight, I loitered about the interior of the cathedral while evensong proceeded beyond the narrow entrance of the choir, allowing me, from the dimmer recesses of the nave, suggestive glimpses of surplices, shaded lamps, anthem sheets and musical motions within. It was magical. The rest of the great building lay in hush, haunted only by self-consciously shuffling groups of sightseers, and encapsulated there in their bright-lit chamber, as though in heavenly orbit, the Dean, his canons, the musicians and a handful of devoted worshippers performed their evening ritual.

The anthem was S.S. Wesley's *Thou Wilt Keep Him,* among the most lyrical in the repertoire, and it was touching to see how many of the tourists leant in silence against pillars, or paused thoughtfully in their decipherment of epitaphs, as the sweet melody sounded through the half-light.

– o / o / o –

"Can I go and meet Daddy now?" I heard a voice say from the cathedral shop, near the west door (where Mr. John Harvey's work seemed to be selling well). "He's bound to be down from the loft by now." He was, the last note of the voluntary having faded away into the Lady Chapel, and presently the Organist and Choirmaster, his wife, his two daughters and I were comfortably before a fire in Vicars' Close, the exquisite double row of fourteenth-century houses which runs away to the north of the

Chapter House (and which is the only part of the Wells cathedral precinct properly called the Close). Here was Barchester all right! An Oxford print hung above the fireplace; a cat luxuriated on the hearth; books, musical instruments, edibles and Cinzano were all equally at hand. "Aren't we lucky?" said the children. "Don't we live in a lovely place? Isn't this a lovely house? We tidied it all up specially for you!"

It was by no means the only musical house in the neighborhood, for the cathedral precinct of Wells, if it sometimes suggests show business, and often package tours, sometimes feels like one gigantic conservatoire. Muffled from within the cathedral walls, any hour of the day, one may hear the organ rumbling. Celestial through the open doors come snatches of *Thou Wilt Keep Him*. From old grey houses around the green sound snatches of string quartet, trombonic arpeggios or tinkles of Czerny. Hardly has the Organist and Choirmaster finished one performance than he is up there again with his choristers, high in their medieval practice room behind Penniless Porch, rehearsing Wood in C Minor for the following day.

If faith is the reason for Wells, music is its most obvious diligence. Wells Cathedral School is one of the three schools in England offering specialist education for musically gifted children, tracing its origins to a Song School of the thirteenth century, while the music of the cathedral itself is intensely professional. I much enjoyed this feeling of disinterested technique, so remote from commercial competition or union claim. I saw something truly noble to the spectacle of that daily choral celebration, performed to the last degree of excellence, attended by almost nobody but the celebrants themselves: a practice more generous, more frank, more *English* (I ventured to suppose) than monasticism or meditation—and more acceptable actually, one might think, to the sort of gods I myself cherish, the gods of the stones and the lavender, than to the Christian divinity to whom it has, for a thousand years, uninterruptedly been offered.

Before I left Vicars' Close, the children invited me to write something in their autograph books. Visitors always did, they said. I looked with interest at the previous entries, expecting to find there, as one would in a Barchester book, the names of visiting politicians, magnates or men of law: but no, they were musicians almost to a scrawl—the composers, the instrumentalists, the teachers who pass in a constant stream these days through the busy precincts of Wells. (When I saw what witty things they had written there, I could think of nothing comparably pithy to say myself, so I drew a couple of pictures of the cathedral instead. "Thought you said you couldn't draw," the children kindly said. "We think you're *jolly good.*")

–o/o/o–

The loyalty essential to the myth of Englishness is of course embodied in Wells in the fabric of the cathedral itself, and the enclosure of grass, garden and old stone that surrounds it. For a millennium there have been people in Wells who have devoted themselves to this structure, and it seemed to me that this corporate possession of the little town, like some grand totem or fetish, must powerfully augment the citizenry's sense of community or comradeship.

In a marvellous clutter of sheds, blueprints and piles of stone, tucked away behind the cloisters, works the Master-Mason of the cathedral, Mr. Bert Wheeler. Everybody in Wells, Town or Close, knows Mr. Wheeler. "You've seen Bert Wheeler?" they used to ask me almost anxiously, lest I might have missed him, and if I quoted his opinion on something, the age of an arch, the angle of a subsidence, all argument was stilled. Mr. Wheeler has been associated with Wells Cathedral, first as choirboy, then as mason, since 1933, and there is hardly an inch of the fabric that he has not befriended.

How easy it would be, I thought, to fall in love with such a building, and to spend one's life getting to know it, or more usefully perhaps, keeping it there! In the shadow of such permanence, surely life's transient miseries would pass one by? The Master-Mason smiled enigmatically: he is a very practical man. He first fell victim himself to the enthrallment of the cathedral when as a small boy he wriggled through a prohibited aperture somewhere in the masonry, and so discovered for himself the infinite complexity of the place. Now he knows it all, its unsuspected corridors and hidden galleries, its vaults and its cloisters, and through his yards and offices pass all the architects, the restorers, the masons, the accountants, the surveyors and the builders' merchants perpetually engaged, as they have been for so many centuries, in maintaining the holy structure. He was like the Master-at-Arms on a warship, I thought, beneath whose experienced eye the workaday life of the vessel goes on, leaving the men on the bridge above, like those priests and choristers at evensong, free to attend to the navigation.

Then there is the Horologist. The most beloved single artifact in Wells Cathedral, I would say, is the medieval Great Clock in the north transept. It is claimed to possess the oldest working clock in Europe: whenever it strikes the hour four little horsemen, whirring round and round, knock each other off their wooden horses with lances, while a dead-pan character called Jack Blandiver, sitting stiffly on his seat high on a wall near by, nods his head, hits one bell with a hammer, and kicks two more with his heels.

Every morning at half past eight or so, if you hang around High Street, you may see Mr. Ken Fisher of Fisher's the Clockmakers, on his way to wind this endearing timepiece. His father did it before him, his son will doubtless follow, and never was a labor more cherished. "There's old Jack," says Mr. Fisher affectionately as he unlocks the door to the clock gantry, and looks up at the quaint old figure on the wall: and when you have climbed the narrow winding steps, looking through the inverted arches to the empty nave beyond, then he opens the big glass doors of the mechanism as one might open a cabinet of treasures.

The works are Victorian, the originals being in the Science Museum at South Kensington, and Mr. Fisher admires them enormously. What workmanship! What precision! Look at those cogs! Feel how easily the handle turns! (There are three separate movements to be wound up each morning, with a big iron handle, and Mr. Fisher is not averse to his visitors helping with the work.) I caught his mood at once, and found the experience oddly soothing. Everything felt wonderfully *handmade* up there, so rich in old wood and dressed stone, with that elaborate gleaming mechanism slowly ticking, and Mr. Fisher in his shirt-sleeves admiring it, and the beautiful cool space of the cathedral beneath one's feet.

"Wouldn't it be good," I said, "if *everything* in life felt like this?" "Ah wouldn't it," said he, resuming his coat after the exertion of the clock-winding. "But you have to work for it, you see. It doesn't look after itself! Come here now, look down here"—and he showed me down a little shaft to the circular platform on which the four knights of the Great Clock, relieved from their eternal joust until the next quarter-hour, were resting woodenly on their arms. "Now those fellows down there take a lot of looking after. They break so easily, you see. Well they would, wouldn't they, hitting each other with their lances every quarter of an hour? You can't expect them to last for ever, knocking each other about like that!"

−o / o / o−

In a curious way, I felt, the cathedral was more the property of the Town than of the Close. Bishops, Deans and Canons come and go (only three Deans have gone on to be Bishops of Bath and Wells), but the shop-keepers and the businessmen, the farmers, even the traders who bring their vans and stalls to Wells Market every week—these people live all their lives in the presence of the great building, and must feel it to be part of their very selves. Wells has its own magnificent parish church of St. Cuthbert, often mistaken by the tourists for the cathedral itself. It has a substantial landed interest and some thriving small industries. But still every street seems to look, every alley seems to lead, almost every con-versation seems somehow to turn, to that ancient presence beyond Penni-less Porch.

To discover how jealously Wellensians, as citizens of Wells compli-catedly call themselves, regard the affairs of the Close, I went to see the newspaper editor. Like nearly everything in Wells, his office is only a step or two from the cathedral, almost opposite the Star (and just up the road from the King's Head which has been unnervingly metamorphosed into a Chinese restaurant). The paper is shortly to move to more modern premises, but its funny old gimcrack buildings are for the moment in High Street, all ramshackle and disjointed, like the kitchen quarters of some dilapidated mansion. How knowingly, I thought, those Linotypes chattered! What intrigues, vendettas and innuendos had found their way through those presses, during the 128 years in which the *Wells Journal* has kept its eye impartially on precinct and marketplace!

Ah yes, said the editor wryly. There was never a shortage of gossip in Wells, or controversy either. They were an independent sort, the Wellen-sians. Why, I should have heard the fuss when the Bishop took to culling the wild duck in his moat by shooting them out of his window! Or when they built those dreadful new canons' houses, all trendy streaked con-crete, behind the Old Deanery! Oh, yes, Wellensians often resented the airs of the clergymen Up There: though it was not strictly true that the precinct was walled in defence against the assaults of the townspeople, often enough it felt like it.

The Alderman vehemently agreed—the controversial Alderman, every-one called him, who turned out to be a fiery Welshman, bred by the Parachute Regiment out of the Swansea valleys, whose passionately conservationist views during his period as Mayor had led him into bitter conflict with the cathedral. Vividly he recalled those old affrays for me. Had he not threatened to take the Dean to court when he chopped down the Mulberry Tree? Did he not lead the opposition to those frightful canonical houses? Was it not he who instructed his Council, when the Bishop was late for a civic function, to take their seats without his Lordship?

The Alderman clearly loves a fight, and I rather wished he was engaged in one just then, so that I could see the sparks fly for myself. But no, though he spoke to me movingly of an erroneous new sewage scheme, all was quiet in Wells just then. There had been a new Bishop and a new Dean since his mayoral days, and most of the local government functions had been taken away to Shepton Mallet anyway. He sounded rather disappointed, and so was I; for Barchester is not Barchester, after all, without a battle on its hands.

– o / o / o –

Or, for that matter, without a Mrs. Proudie. It was when I reached the Bishopric at last that I felt my pilgrimage had failed. Faith I had certainly found in Wells, diligence, loyalty, pride: but the sense of authority, of an established order unbreakable and supreme, which is essential to the Romantic view of England, is lost with the winds of social change and historical necessity. In Trollope's allegories that old discipline was represented if not by the person, at least by the office of the Bishop, splendidly identified by his accoutrements, his circumstances and his privileges; but the Anglican Bishop of tradition, gloriously fortified by material well-being and spiritual complacency—that grand figure of fancy has long gone the way of the Empire-builder and the top-hatted Station Master.

As it happens the Bishop's Palace at Wells is perhaps the most splendid Bishop's Palace of all. Surrounded by its own moat, its own castellated walls, its own parkland beyond, it stands on the edge of Wells, in the flank of the cathedral, looking across green fields into the depths of Somerset. It is like a fortress, and though the enormous banqueting hall is now only a picturesque ruin, still the palace is a terrific spectacle. Duck of many varieties paddle its moat, and swans deftly ring the gatehouse bell for their victuals. The palace itself stands grandly around its yard, with a huge pillared refectory, and a fine library, and a private chapel in which, within living memory, daily choral services were held for the Bishop, his family and his servants.

But no majestically awful Mrs. Proudie greeted me at the palace door. Nobody greeted me at the main door at all, for the Bishop of Bath and Wells now lives only in the north wing of the structure, the rest being devoted to conferences and other useful activities. Gone are the days when the Bishop and his family ate all alone in splendor in the center of the vast undercroft, surveyed by a gigantic gilded mitre above the fireplace. Gone are those daily services in the private chapel—nowadays the Bishop prays there alone. Gone is the daunting approach to the episcopal Presence, never to be forgotten by curates of long ago, when after treading the long stately corridors of the palace, through the dark gallery lined with portraits of earlier prelates, they timidly opened the door of the great study to discover his Lordship, against a serried background of the theological treatises, tremendously at his labors.

The Bishop himself recalled that vanished consequence for me. Now he and his distinctly un-Proudean wife live more modestly, more sensibly no doubt, more Christianly I suppose, but undeniably less impressively in their nicely done-up wing. His new study, furnished in pale woodwork by the Church Commissioners, is unexpectedly emblazoned, around the tops of its bookcases, with a text not from Leviticus or the Sermon on the Mount, but from King Alfred. His visitors' book, when I signed it, contained on the previous page the signature of Peter O'Toole. His car is a Rover—"such a blessing when you're overtaking on our narrow Somerset roads." This is a very modern, very functional bishopric.

For here at the core the times have overtaken Barchester. The majesty has left the palace. Crowds of people throng to those conference rooms, taking their cafeteria luncheons on canteen tables in the undercroft (where the gilded mitre looms large as ever, but anomalous). Often the gardens are open to the public, and at any time of day sightseers are to be observed hanging over the gate which, inside the great gatehouse above the moat, inadequately (to my mind) asserts the privacy of the bishopric.

Nobody could represent these changes more persuasively than the present Bishop and his wife, who sit in their modest private corner of the gardens as a Bishop and his lady should, relishing the green and the grey of it all, the long mellow line of their ancient wall, the sweep of the trees and the droop of the trumpet vine, the Turneresque pile of the ruined banqueting hall, the silent towers of the cathedral beyond. But it is not the same. Atavist that I am, yearning sometimes from the austerity of Wales for some of the gorgeous and heedless assurance that used to characterize our magnificent neighbor—nostalgic in this way for the England I am just old enough to remember, I missed the purple swagger and the swank.

For it was partly the conceit of it, Trollope's hubris of the cloth, that captured our imaginations once—now gone it seems, for better or for worse, as utterly from Barchester as from Simla or Singapore.

Thums Up

AN INDIAN JOURNEY

I sit on my balcony in the Taj Mahal Hotel, Bombay, one of the best hotels in the world, eating my breakfast, fending off the occasional crow and watching the kaleidoscopic scene below me: the swarming white figures on the waterfront, hastening here and there, clustered in conspiratorial knots, doing calisthenics on the lawns; the ships scattered across the great bay beyond; the dim blue hills of the mainland across the water; the docks and merchant houses and factory chimneys running away up the coast to Manul and Trombay. I arrived in India in the small hours of this morning, and I am easing myself in. There is not a shack to be seen from up here, or an open drain, let alone a corpse; the only scavengers around are those irrepressible birds, and the beggars assembling for the day's work in the street below are, if not quite out of sight, at least more or less out of mind.

I always do it this way, and though cosmopolitans and retired hippies accuse me of escapism, and think I ought to stay my first night in a Vegetarian Boarding-House or better still an ashram, the device has served well in the past to coddle me through the discomforts of culture lag. This time, though, it does not work so well. Even up there in my balcony, a premonition nags at me, a niggle at the senses, for something has perceptibly changed in the scene below. For twenty years and more the view from the Taj has looked to me more or less changeless, but this time there is a difference. The buildings are the same, the freighters seem scarcely to have moved, the same old Indian aircraft-carrier is still undergoing its apparently permanent re-fit at the naval quay. The change, it gradually dawns upon me over the chilled orange juice, is this: that those white swarming figures below me on the waterfront have quite palpably multiplied.

There is a ghost story by M. R. James in which shrouded figures in an ancient painting are terrifyingly discovered to be moving, year by year, towards some unrevealed horror. I am reminded of it now by the change in the view from the Taj, but I am not imagining things. Since I was last in Bombay, in 1977, India's population has increased by at least thirty million—as though the entire populations of Venezuela and Colombia were to have migrated here. It has increased by at least a third since I first came to this city, in 1953. It is increasing this month by a million, and Bombay's own population is expected to have doubled by the end of the century. No wonder I notice something happening down there: India is the one place in the world where, rather as in a slow motion movie of some natural process, the eruption of an earthquake, the rise of a tide, the habitual visitor may see the statistics actually occurring, there before one's eyes, over papaya and scrambled egg on the hotel balcony.

Everywhere I went, during my visit to India in the summer of 1980, I did not merely sense, but actually observed the population growing. Any street scene, any rural road demonstrates it. The sidewalks are tangibly more packed, the buses audibly more overloaded, the railway trains more alarmingly scrambled over by desperate commuters, the country roads more jammed than ever with carts and bicycles and half-derelict trucks and knots of women with pots on their heads and cows and ruminative goats and swarms of naked children and old men asleep in the shade of banyan trees and beggars apparently dead, their sticks still in their hands, flat on their backs in the gutter dust.

I got used to it of course, as usual. One gets used to everything in India, especially when the terrible hot weather marches inexorably, day by day, feverish and sweaty like some universal plague towards the cataclysm of the monsoon. We all know the stab of conscience, one of the oldest hazards of Indian travel, that distresses us for a moment when we drive away the 38th beggar-mother of the morning: but most of us rationalize our inhumanity in the end—it's not our fault, it's not our country, didn't you know the beggars had a syndicate of their own? "We pay our servants well," one of the sleeker foreign consuls told me, "and that is duty done."

And the easiest escape of all, anyway, is offered by the example of the

Indians themselves. Svelte and soignée in the Western-style restaurants, any day of the week, young Bombay flaunts its wealth and its sophistication, discussing the Manhattan movies of only the day before yesterday, quoting the *New Statesman* before last on the Afghan situation or reminiscing piercingly about that nice little boutique just above Sunset Boulevard, you know, past the Hyatt. Electronically attended in air-conditioned penthouse suites, being offered cool gins-and-tonics by silent attendants on exquisite roof-gardens, across the downtown city the brilliant industrialists and entrepreneurs of Bombay enjoy the fruit of their acumen. Poor people in their thousands have erected tattered bustee-homes, bits of canvas strung together, old boxes propped one against the other, against the wall of the Bombay racecourse: but just over the wall, as in some vicious allegory, or rather too obvious propaganda picture, the sleek and lovely thoroughbreds are fed their daily vitamins.

"My husband says," observes an Indian friend of mine, tucking into the buffet luncheon at the rococo-splendid Oberoi, while the fountains splash cool and soothing in the indoor grotto—"my husband says that I shouldn't bring foreign visitors to places like this. He says it gives a false impression." "Well he's right," I say, "next time we'll meet at the street stall outside the railway station." But of course we won't. The trouble with India, Nehru thought, was that its practice never matched its principle, but I disagree: the trouble is the principle. Privilege and inequality are part of the Indian scheme of things, immemorial, ineradicable I think. You are in, or you are out. You know nobody, you know everyone. How, I wondered, could I get inside the naval dockyard of Bombay, whose Victorian architecture I thought might interest me? My companion looked surprised that I should even bother to ask. "Have a word with the Admiral," she replied.

Have a word with the Admiral! There is something to the very intonation of India that seems to imprison this country in its own caricature—more unfair, more hopeless, more unchangeable, more pathetic, more provoking, more endearing, more ominous than any other on the face of the globe. Why is India like it is? Because of religion, says one sage. Because of irreligion, says another. Because of climate, or politics, or history, or geography, or ignorance, or hunger, or imperialism, or capitalism or human nature!

Human nature certainly. India is more human than anywhere else. It is human two or three times over, and more so every month. There is no

affliction of India, from avarice to leprosy, in which we cannot see ourselves reflected. The miseries of caste are only class consciousness, or ra-
cialism, interpreted another way. The awful contrasts of Indian life can
be seen in little, watered down, anywhere in the Western world. India is
our mirror, or perhaps our crystal ball: the disturbing insight I got on
my balcony that breakfast-time—dear God, was it a prophecy for us all, a
glimpse of chaos coming? "Time we had a war," somebody said to me in
Bombay. "War is a cleanser of things."

$$-o/o/o-$$

I did not have a word with the Admiral, but I did call on the Governor's
wife, in her seaside palace above the sea. She is a kind, composed and
exact lady, like the headmistress of a sensibly disciplined girls' school, and
suggested that I might like to walk around the estate, which rambles
agreeably, in a succession of white bungalows, up and down the rocks at
the end of the Malabar peninsula (and harbors also, incidentally, a shrine
to the goddess Khiva frequented by fishermen on their way to work, but
infested with plainclothes policemen when I was there, owing to an
impending visit by Mrs. Gandhi).

Among the wooded lanes I came across a pets' cemetery, established by
gubernatorial predecessors long ago, in which a number of dead dogs
were sentimentally commemorated with texts and headstones. Here is
the epitaph I liked the best:

LINDY LOO

1932–1943

HER TAIL STILL WAGS

IN OUR HEARTS

$$-o/o/o-$$

Everyone said I should take the little rack railway for my trip to Ootacamund, "Snooty Ooty," the well-beloved hill station in the Nilgiri Hills,
where the game of snooker was invented, and the annual flower show is
one of the posher events of the Indian season. I am relatively impervious
to the allure of steam, though, and the last thing I wanted was nostalgia.
So I took a car instead, and we wound quite majestically up the forest
road, swerving sometimes to avoid the more torpid local apes, and scrupu-
lously obeying the genteel traffic signs along the way—AVOID OVER-SPEED-
ING, or BE COURTEOUS TO FELLOW-DRIVER.

But it was nostalgia I got anyway. Once the favorite resort of Victorian imperialists, Ooty nowadays is a paradise of the Bombay and Madrasi bourgeoisie, and I was passed from villa to villa, introduction to introduction, rather as a foreign visitor might have been handed from one house party to another, I imagine, in Edwardian Newport. Witty dames in diamond nose-clips gave me tea and gossip. Parsee families escaping the lowland heat looked up from their Monopoly boards and embroidery frames to ask after dear Benjy, Dodo or Binky. At the races (where I lost 30 rupees on Mr. Kanwar Manjitinder Singh's Apple Pudding) the swells of the Madras Race Club, in headscarves and check caps, sat in their grandstand marking their race cards for all the world like extras in a very late-night English movie.

I stayed at the elderly Savoy Hotel, encouched in gardens on a hillside, and as I whiled the hours away sketching beneath its gum trees among the phlox it occurred to me that nothing had really happened to Ooty, this haven of drawing-room values, for half a century or more. There were new factories and housing estates on the outskirts of town, but its essence remained absolutely unaltered—even the demography is invisible, in this well-hedged and comfortable enclave. Potted geraniums thrived as always beneath the portes-cochères of gabled villas. The Ooty Club bristled still with the assorted heads of jackals and Masters of the Hunt (the ones stuffed, the others oil-painted). The Nilgiri Library suggested to me the ship's library of the *Marie Celeste*—frozen, it seemed, intact, unaltered, since the departure of its last Victorian subscribers.

I would have known it all from the pictures in the old travel books. There were the wandering cows, engraved against the hillsides just as they always were, and there were the statutory picturesque women still toiling up the lanes with their bundles and babies. Every now and then, from behind my back, one of the hotel ponies burst wildly into view, small child clamped resolutely in its saddle, groom panting behind in respectfully buttoned jacket, and sometimes the nursemaid from the next bungalow wandered by, carrying the family infant—"Morning *ayah*," I would say, doing as the Romans do, and "Morning Auntie," she habitually replied.

Nothing has changed; nothing is new; nothing is fresh; nothing, actually, is original. Like so much else in India, Ooty is only a rather stale copy of an alien pattern: it is one of the sadnesses of the country that its people are *still* copying, after forty years of independence, and are still stuck in a sterile equilibrium between East and West. All the most important newspapers in India are published in English. Yet it is half-cock English, stilted and ungainly, less precise, more muddled every time I go, and so an ever less effective instrument of government or instruction ("You take the first-class on the right," a man in Bombay told me beguilingly, when I asked the way to Marine Drive, "and that will take you straight to Marendrav").

Indian capitalism slavishly follows the forms of the West, from hotel menus ("Mouth-Watering Delicacies From Out the Blue Arabian Sea") to sententious displays ("Erected by S.R.Mukkerjee Ltd In the Interests of Municipal Improvement") to advertising hyperboles ("NEW!!! THE TOOTHPASTE OF THE STARS!"). A number of Indian painters were asked recently to talk about their art, and their responses would have been all too familiar to connoisseurs of the art-trade baloney—"My art gives me a feeling of the particular thingness of a thing"—"What I endeavour to express is the opposite polarities of black and white."

Only India suffers, in the same degree anyway, from this stifling cultural legacy, and it makes for a sad stagnancy, however vigorously the indigenous cultures, the native art forms, struggle away behind the façade. Ooty exemplifies it, in its gentle and pleasurable way, and after a few days in the town I began to think that the only truly liberated people around were the Todas, an enigmatic aboriginal folk who live with their buffalos in the surrounding hills.

Nobody knows the ethnic origins of these people—some scholars believe them to have Greek or Roman blood—and they are physically unlike any other Indians anywhere. I went to visit a group of them. They no longer occupied their traditional huts, which look something like enormous dog kennels, and something like lime kilns, but they had kept one to serve as a temple for their somewhat obscure religious rites, and there the headman assembled a few of his tribespeople to meet me. They were splendid-looking people, tall, gaunt, taciturn, with long patrician faces like horses or dukes, and lean scholarly bodies, like historians. One or two had hastily assumed their hereditary costume, a truly Augustan toga, and they stood around me in grandiose poses, like statues in a forum. I thought they were much the poshest people in Ootacamund, the only ones who seemed to honor their own origins to the full: but when I left their encampment, and drove away through the eucalyptus woods, an infant Toda toddled desperately after my car, waving a long, agitated but rather wistful goodbye—all down the dappled forest lane, waving all the way, until he was hardly more than a little black gesturing speck, far back between the trees. "He wants to come with us," I said. "Can you wonder?" my companion replied. "Four years is quite long enough to be a Toda."

—o / o / o—

Wandering around the purlieus of the High Court in Madras, a prodigy of red-brick domes, turrets and galleries, with a disused lighthouse mounted theatrically on top of it, I took out my cassette recorder to remind myself of some of its architectural peculiarities. At once I heard an admonitory clapping of the hands, the Indian equivalent of "Hey, you!", and a policeman with a night-stick—*lathi* in the vernacular—beckoned me over.

"What have you got there? What is this machine?"

"It's a tape recorder."

"What are you doing with it here?"

"I am reminding myself of some architectural peculiarities."

"How do I know it is not a bomb?"

"You can speak into it yourself."

"What shall I say?"

"Anything."

"I cannot think of anything to say."

"Sing a song then."

"What kind of a song?"

"A Tamil song."

"Very well, I will sing you a very old Tamil song, a tragic song"—and half-closing his eyes, and assuming an unmistakably tragic expression, there in the sunshine outside the court in a high wavering voice he sang several verses of a very, very old Tamil song. I played it back to him.

"Very well," he said, "now you have my voice. What will you give me in return? What part of you may I keep in exchange?"

But bless his heart, I was gone by then.

–o / o / o–

In Cochin, on the southwest coast, I bought a Japanese 35mm color film. This was an achievement. Foreign-made goods are exceedingly hard to come by in provincial India, and one must generally make do with local substitutes. My film had probably been smuggled ashore from a foreign ship in port, and buying it gave me, just for a moment, a stinging, shot-in-the-arm sensation. How modern it looked, and bright! How clean and crisp its packaging! How confident it made me feel that it would work! One misses these things in India, a place of brownish, greyish, ill-printed objects, cars designed a generation ago, books that split in the binding, black, white and speckled television, crossed telephone lines and mislaid bookings.

But in Cochin I felt that it need not be so. Cochin is the chief city of Kerala, which was the first Indian State to go Communist, but of all the Indian cities it seems to me the most vivaciously free of spirit. It consists of a clutch of ancient settlements scattered around a network of inlets from the Arabian Sea, but it was transformed in the 1940s by the creation of a new harbor, and is now the fifth port of India. An artificial island, thrown up by the dredging of the harbor, is now the true center of the old city-complex, and the tip of it, beside the anomalously neo-classic offices of the Port Trust, is the best place to go to get the hang of it.

There is a pavilion down there, right at the water's edge, and before it the harbor is displayed rather like an Experience in an exhibition. By Indian standards it is a positively effervescent scene. Big ships stalk in from the open sea, dug-out canoes scud by under tattered sails, lumpish barges are plied laboriously from one quay to another, tugs and pilot launches pompously pass, motor-ferries make noises like the prolonged blowing of raspberries, a thousand fishing-boats, or so it seems, rush in and out of harbor at perpetual full speed, foaming at the prow, as if they are only just in time to pounce upon a passing shoal, or catch a closing market. Dolphins often leap and crest in the waters out there, and on the other side of the harbor the huge rope contraptions of the shore fishermen, mounted on platforms above the surf, ponderously move up and down in silhouette, rather as oil wells slowly curtsey in Texas or Oklahoma.

This is more like Hong Kong than Bombay, let alone Ooty, and the exuberance extends into the town, too. Cochin is full of it. Hilarious Swedish seamen stagger along Broadway waving whiskey bottles. Jolly shopkeepers shout black-market bargains. There is no prohibition in Kerala, and the local Minister for Land Revenues and Excise is called Mr. Baby John. The colors of the place are the colors of the bright south, and the pace is that intoxicating combination of the frenzied and the complacent that goes with leaping dolphins, bananas, coconuts, trade winds, Baby Johns and all that. It feels a million miles from the halls of the Indian Federal Government, in the far dun plains of New Delhi.

And so, historically, it is. Until 1947, when India achieved independence, Cochin was one of the princely States which had, by one of history's most extraordinary quirks, kept its sovereignty, in form if not in fact, since the Middle Ages. The British never annexed it, only took it under their protection, and accordingly it was never tamed or homogenized. The Portuguese and the Dutch both had ancient trading colonies here, Hindus, Muslims and Christians all proliferated, and the ornate synagogue in Jew Street, floored with precious Chinese tiles and endowed with many curious relics, functions to this day: it is no coincidence that its curator, Mr. Cohen, speaks an English altogether untainted by the usual sing-song of India (despite a grievous loss of teeth in a recent motorscooter accident), for Cochin had remained that rarity among Indian cities, a truly cosmopolitan, open-ended sort of place.

It is the old variety, the repeated infusion of fresh blood, that keeps Cochin so vivid now, and makes one feel more than ever, by contrast, how gagged and helpless Mother India is within her gigantic introspections. For there is no businessman sharper than your Indian, when given half a chance to make a fortune. Wherever they settle in the world outside, Fiji, Manchester, Nairobi, Indian capitalists easily outsmart the local competition, and even within India the great business and industrial dynasties, the Mahratta Birlas, the Parsee Tatas, are a match for their fellow-magnates anywhere, when it comes to innovative enterprise.

Yet the nation struggles along in a miasma of hopelessness. Nothing is getting better. Nothing catches up. The fantastic industrial progress of Singapore, Korea or Taiwan, the new flowering of China, finds no parallel in this elephantine democracy. The electronic revolution ignores it: the silicon chip looks the other way. The dead hand of the Center, applied by agencies nobody can quite elucidate, embodied in doctrines few can define, casts its shadow over every corner of India, and seems to dampen nearly every fire.

Bureaucracy, industrialists say, is why India is like it is, and perhaps they are right. Like a muffle officialdom envelops every Indian initiative, suffocating it in layer upon layer of files, dockets, application forms, permission slips, references, precedents, objections, appeals, postponements, conditions, further inquiries and promises of quick decision after the summer recess. It can take *years* to set up a new Indian factory, before a brick is laid on the ground: and every year, as we remember, there are some 12 million more Indians to keep alive.

In Cochin one day I chanced to see an announcement painted on the back of a motor-rickshaw. HYPOTHECATED TO THE STATE BANK OF INDIA, it said. I took this to mean that the vehicle was in hock against a bank loan, but just to make sure I asked a knowledgeable student of my acquaintance. He didn't know exactly what it meant, either, but had a ready answer nonetheless. Hypothecated, he said, was what we all were. "Hypothecated means they've got you where they want you. I'm hypothecated. You're hypothecated. They hypothecate us all."

−o / o / o−

I arrived at the scene of the accident shortly after the event, and the country road was still half-blocked by the muddle of it. The truck was overturned in the ditch; both the bullock carts were toppled broken on their sides, their big wooden wheels ungainly in the air, their ripped sacks spilling grain across the highway. Three men whom I took to be the drivers were sitting motionless on their haunches at the edge of the road, and under the trees a little huddle of women was talking in a high-pitched but muted gabble, very fast, nervously. An old man in a dhoti walked round and round the wreckage, prodding it with his stick and coughing.

Rivulets of glutinous dark blood ran away down the camber of the road to the gutter, collecting down there in a puddle, a few leaves already floating in it from the trees above. One of the bullocks had been torn open right along its flank, and guts were oozing obscenely from its smooth skin. The other animal was bleeding heavily through the nostrils, and even as I watched it raised its head a little, with a sort of gurgle at the mouth, and then dropped it heavily on to the ground again. The old man prodded it inquisitively with his stick. The three squatters did not stir. "Drive on," I said.

−o / o / o−

Give us a rupee, said the small boys in the courtyard of the Mecca Mosque in Hyderabad, where the Nizams are buried in their stately rows. No, I said. *One rupee,* they said. No rupee. *One rupee.* No rupee. *One rupee.* No rupee. And so, there in that sacred enclosure beneath the minarets, I found myself almost involuntarily dancing to a jig to the rhythm of our exchange, while the urchins, perfectly unabashed, pranced light-footed all around me, and the men sitting in the shade beside the tombs clapped and laughed to see us—*One rupee, no rupee, one rupee, no rupee.* . . .

It is a miracle of India that it remains, for its desperations, a very merry country, a gaudy country, a terrific entertainment. Laughter is easy to come by, like hospitality, even in the stews. The beat of the drum enlivens every evening, and the people's gift for innocent jollity is not dampened yet. Nothing is so festive as an Indian festival. No band is so jaunty as an Indian band, rollicking through the slum-streets in its red and orange uniforms, blowing its tubas lustily. No gamins or mudlarks are more fun to watch than the illegal riders on the Indian commuter trains, perilously leaping on and off with a marvellously debonaire panache. Those two dead bullocks had gaily decorated horns—one pair painted bright blue, the other tipped with brass—and the truck that killed them was painted in a delightfully elaborate design of flowers, animals, scrolls and baroque embellishments. Choc-O-Luv, Blind Love and Frenzi are all popular ice-creams in India, and no folk-art is livelier than an Indian film poster, which characteristically includes a space rocket, a clutch of skyscrapers, a distant view of Kashmir, a group of skin-divers, a submarine, two or three Mercedes cars and a fattish young hero, center front, who, while gazing moistly into the eyes of his beloved, seems to be searching her long black hair for nits.

This is the magnificent innocence of India, which alone, I fear, enables its citizens to survive in decency. For Gandhi it was the great untapped energy of the land. The innocence of truth itself, the simplicity of it, the beauty—this was Power in a specifically Indian kind, a Life-Force to be exploited and harnessed for the national good: and the Great Soul proved that it worked by using it triumphantly to get the British out of India. The fire of the conception died with him, though. The Gandhian philosophy is impotent in India now; the old innocence is force going to waste, like untapped sunshine, or tides.

On a public level the Republic of India is about as innocent as a snake-pit. Its politics are poisoned by rivalries and corruptions that make Watergate seem almost wholesome—or at least comprehensible. Between the lines of the political dispatches a myriad old scores are perpetually being settled, or new splinter groups being arranged, and India is almost always embroiled in the symptoms of party warfare—the inescapable slogans and swapped abuse, the politicians huddled with their aides in the backs of motor-cars, the bicycle-rickshaws with tape-decks on their passenger seats, mindlessly bawling injunctions through the back-streets. Indian graffiti are unmatched for variety and obscurity, like DOWN WITH ENEMY, BEWARE SPIES, OPEN THE COLLEGE THIS INSTANT TO FACE US: even in genteel Ooty I found scrawled in red ink outside the Savoy the incantation HOTEL MANAGEMENT DOWN—DOWN—DOWN—DOWN—and at the bottom there was a primitive cartoon of the hotel manager, drawn with a certain savage elegance, like those of bulls in cave paintings.

Cynicism has always been an Indian virtue, but it has, so my friends tell me, gone too deep today. Nobody believes anything now. There is a way out of everything. A lie lurks behind every truth. And the more the social pressures grow, as each man treads more desperately upon another's heels, the more sour becomes the public mood. The simplicities wilt in despair, and Gandhi's divine vision becomes ever dimmer and more discredited, honored now only by cranks and visionaries, or holy gurus in their sanctuaries. The very cycle of life and death, it seems to me, is wobbling out of true. I did not leave that mosque in Hyderabad until the sun was low behind the minarets, and as the boys and I crossed the great courtyard to the gate I chanced to notice our dancing shadows on the stone. We looked rather eerie in silhouette: my tall and skinny figure elongated in the center, and all around me those capering imps, proceeding in elvish display past the sleeping line of Nizams.

—o / o / o—

There was a time when Patna University was considered to be one of the best universities in India in the matter of discipline and teaching. This record has been spoilt by the murders which have taken place in recent months.

> Spokesman for the Bihar Citizens' Council,
> reported in *The Searchlight,* Patna

—o / o / o—

Even now, thirty years after independence, you cannot escape imperialism in India. Having an interest in its architecture, I decided to take a stroll around the lines of buildings erected in the 1920s and 1930s to house the administrators of the Indian capital, New Delhi. Caste is endemic, infectious too, in this country, and the houses are arranged in inexorable hierarchy—tenements for peons at the bottom, bungalows for civil servants in the middle, a gigantic palace, bigger than Versailles, for the Viceroy of India at the top. I chose a middle category to start with (Grade V in the street directory), and finding a likely example encouched in a nice garden on a street corner, combed my hair and entered its gate.

A plump man in a dhoti was helping himself to a glass of water from a jar on the verandah. "Come in, come in," he said. "What may I do for you? Please sit down! Have a glass of lemonade—the lemons grow in this very garden. Let us talk!" I sneaked a glance at the name on the letter-box by the door, and found him to be Mr. B.J., one of the most powerful Communists, and best-known politicians, in India.

As he went off to the back quarters to arrange the lemonade, arranging his garment around him like a bath towel after swimming, I took a look around his study. So this was the headquarters of an Indian Marxist! I was not surprised, of course, by the complete works of Lenin on a top shelf, or the complicated structure of correspondence trays, stacked rather like the lattice-work of an old-fashioned bridge, which spoke authentically of party committees, national executive councils and People's Conventions. But what was this, over here in the corner? A series of proud pictures of Mr. B.J. himself, dressed very smartly not in Stalinist jacket or Maoist cap, but in the uniform of a British Army officer, amidst a smiling crowd of jolly decent looking English soldiers on some very obviously English heath!

He was not at all put out, when he returned with the drinks, to find me pondering these snapshots. On the contrary, he told me all about his career as a British officer, his training at Camberley in the heathlands of Surrey, his brother now settled in Sussex, his doubts about Mrs. Thatcher, his fears for the future of the Old Country—for all the world, I thought, as though he were himself a settler in the East, looking back nostalgically to the country of his origins.

It is popular still, even among many Indians, to view with complacency the continuing Britishness of the Indian system, despite all odds. Only the British-founded Civil Service, they say, could have brought India through so many troubles. Only the British-inspired Indian Army could have preserved its security. And is it not gratifying, Britons especially like to say, to see pictures of old white Governors still *in situ* on official walls, or better still, group portraits of Staff College course members above the mantelpieces of New Delhi Communists?

I take an opposite view. That engaging familiarity with the English scene somehow weakened B.J. in my eyes, for all his civilized hospitality, just as the inescapable relics of British method seem to me to debilitate this Asian nation, set beside the styles and loyalties of China or Japan. Of course it is aesthetically interesting to see the remains of the Raj still apparent among the crumbled castles, the deserted capitals, the mosques and temples of their predecessors. They add a new and often elegant dimension to the inconceivable richness of India. The stunning Victorian buildings of Bombay, towering there in their flamboyant mixture of Gothic, Muslim and Hindu, ecclesiastical and secular, commanding and conciliatory, will one day join the Taj and the ruins of Fatephur Sikri, I do not doubt, as symbols on tourist posters. And few experiences of modern travel are more historically suggestive than a drink on the terrace of the Adyar Club in Madras, gleaming white above the Adyar River, with its green gardens all around and the garden bench mounted high in its classical cupola to catch the fresh breezes off the sea—the perfect English colonial house, still comfortable in the English kind, still graced by touches of English eccentricity, but long ago left high and dry among its tennis courts by history's shifting course.

But as to Britishness in less substantial forms, it seems to me an Indian curse. Systems which may have been progressive in Edwardian times still linger on, ever more bedraggled and outdated. The powerful Federal Government at the center, once an instrument of imperial stability, remains an instrument of reaction, for ever preserving the *status quo,* stifling always, one after the other, the movements for change which bubble down the years from Assam to Kashmir. If there has not been a revolution in India, sweeping away to a fresh start, it is because the ghosts of the British are lingering still around the halls of Indian Government.

Even the manners of imperialism balefully survive. In Patna I had occasion to go to the Secretariat to get permission to take photographs of the city (it is one of the many paranoias of Indian officialdom that photography of buildings is *per se* a threat to national security). Through successive stockades of governmental rudeness I approached this modest consummation: arrogant soldiers at the gate, loutish watchmen at the door, surly secretaries in outer offices, and at the top of the ladder, slouched over his desk, a functionary of such classic insolence, such an unassailable mixture of resentment, patronage, self-satisfaction and effrontery, that for a moment I felt like picking up his ink-well and throwing it at him.

But I bit my lip and restrained myself, under my breath, with a cautionary quotation from Kipling—

> . . . *the end of the fight is a tombstone white, with the name of the late deceased,*
> *And the epitaph dear: A fool lies here who tried to hustle the East.*

Besides, as I glared at him there, scales dropped from my eyes: his image blurred and reassembled before me, his color paled somewhat, and I saw before my eyes his true archetype and inspiration, the lesser English civil servant—now, as in imperial times, the insufferable master of his art. The bore is father to the babu. I thanked the man profusely, and assured him that I understood *perfectly* why I would have to make an application in triplicate to the Divisional Officer, who would unfortunately not be on duty until the following Wednesday afternoon.

Or, as the bureaucrats say, words to that effect.

−o / o / o−

Visions come frequently in India, I find, just as perceptions are always clouding, clearing, and clouding again. In Patna one sultry steaming night I was awoken by a colossal clap of thunder, an inch or two, it seemed, from the head of my bed. Simultaneously there was a sound as of Niagara being emptied on to the ceiling, and a blinding series of flashes through the chinks of my drawn curtains, as though the artillery were opening up before the great offensive. The whole city seemed to be rocked by the storm, the noise of it, the eerie lights, the mad rush and beat of the water. When I tried to turn my light on, I found the electricity had failed, and going to the window I found that the entire city was plunged in darkness. There was not an electric light to be seen, not even a headlight. It was as though all life had been obliterated out there, leaving me the only survivor.

But then in the flash of the lightning I saw an eerie sight. Rushing about the half-flooded streets were scores of great white shapes, jostling and splashing crazily through the water. I could not see them clearly,

even when the lightning flashed, but I was left with a writhing, struggling, slippery image of Things out there in the darkness. Heaven help
us all, I thought for a moment, what horror now, to fall upon this tor-
tured country! But then the street lights came on again, and I saw only
the holy cows of Patna, tossing their horns in panic, and wildly milling
around the town.

–o / o / o–

Self-appointed, ingratiating, beyond rebuff, the Bengali attended me down
the shady arcade at noon-day. His grin was beguiling but delusory, for if
it was partly charm and sly humor, it was partly a native toothiness, and
partly I fear emaciation. He was vigorous enough, though. Officiously he
dismissed the shopkeepers who, emerging like rabbits from their burrows
as I passed, clamorously urged me to inspect their carpets, saris, ivory
trinkets or brass trays engraved with images of Agra. Enthusiastically he
ushered me down the corridor towards the blinding oblong of sunshine
at the end—"You want to see anything madam? I can fix it. You want to
buy cheap souvenirs? You want to sightsee anything? Here madam, take
my card, I am always available. . . ."

But when we approached the end of the arcade, he hastened slightly
ahead of me, and stood there bowing and grinning as though to usher me
into another world: and when I caught up with him, and looked out at
the street-scene beyond, I found that he was presenting to me, like some
Dantean major-domo, an authentic glimpse of Hell.

Across the street they were digging something up, so that huge piles of
grey earth gave to the scene, framed still in the dark shadows of the arcade, a background of volcano-like sterility, as though everything beyond
were dead. The street itself was all but motionless, for its traffic was
jammed absolutely solid, apparently for ever: nose to tail its ancient vehicles stood helplessly there, lop-sided double-decker buses and sagging
taxis, the heat shimmering from their roofs: drivers leant from their windows to get a breath of stagnant air, their foreheads dripping sweat, while
the passengers in the buses, upstairs and down, were squeezed so tight
that they could not stand properly, but were curiously distorted this way
and that like figures in medieval manuscripts.

And before me, at my feet, kept at bay now by my ever-smiling cice-
rone, figures straight from the inferno, Bosch figures, scuttled, staggered
and leapt to greet me—men without faces, boys with crumpled feet,

women clutching babies like little bald monkeys, old men who seemed to have risen from the grave, children who whined and plucked my sleeve, and scratched my forearm with filthy nails. "Away, away!" the Bengali cried, smiling and bowing still, and so, cringing a little, closing my eyes and ears, I took the plunge into the sunshine, and went walking in Calcutta.

I wish I could be original about the experience. I wish I could say something new. But Calcutta is always Calcutta: it only gets more so. The streets get dirtier, bumpier, fuller. The bustees press ever more terribly into the business streets and the suburbs. The rich men's houses in their walled gardens seem ever more beleaguered. The power cuts come more often and last longer—twelve hours each day on average this summer, and sometimes sixteen ("Milton's mournful gloom," *The Statesman* called it, in its literary way).

Nobody can staunch it. The great park of the Maidan gets browner and more scuffed. The Hooghly River silts up year by year. The civic buildings crumble in rubble and excrement, while swarms of indigent families, counting their blessings, camp in their once-elegant basements, or lie about their colonnades. Even the saintly Mother Theresa, in her shabby house of mercy on the Lower Circular Road, can do nothing new in Calcutta, only comfort the dying as they leave.

So I will end with three pictures of a familiar kind—perennial pictures from this metropolis of the damned. The first is a cameo. An elderly, frail and respectable-looking man tries to cross a street. He ventures off the sidewalk into the stream of the traffic, and holds up his hand in a gesture at once appealing and a little grand, as though some remnant of old authority sustains him. He seems to demand, as if by right, the deference that age, weakness and dignity deserve, but nobody takes the slightest notice of him. The traffic does not even waver. The taxis do not even hoot. In Calcutta such a man could not stop a baby in a perambulator: and in a trice, sure enough, he is back on the pavement, angrily waiting for another chance, and muttering into his beard.

The second picture is a spectacle: the Hooghly Bridge, still the only bridge across the river in a city of 11 million people, at the end of the day. It is a burly bridge, but in the sunset it seems almost to sag with the burden of its traffic, its multitudes of pedestrians jamming the sidewalks, its long lines of buffalos, wagons, rickshaws, bicycles, buses and trucks. It is a truly tragic spectacle, as the darkness falls: it looks as though a broken army is in retreat westwards across the river, or a great horde of refugees is streaming they know not where, escaping some threatened catastrophe, a plague perhaps, or a holocaust.

And the third picture is just a graffito on a wall. Calcutta never sleeps or pauses, but there is one instance in this city's life when a sudden hush, like the ominous still we read about in the hearts of hurricanes, falls unexpectedly upon the traveller. It is the moment when the taxi-driver, approaching a red traffic light, switches off his engine to save gas. All around the other vehicles have done the same, and so just for a moment, while the roar of the city proceeds beyond the intersection, you are isolated there in a little chamber of quiet—rather like being in a confessional.

Sitting thus one night, my perceptions abruptly awakened by the silence, I noticed a graffito on a nearby wall, gloomily illuminated by the street-lights. This is what it said, in a carefully florid black script:

INDIA SINKS

– o / o / o –

I am drinking a Thums Up Cola, and simultaneously eating an ice-cream, on the river embankment in the evening. Huge crowds wander along the river paths. Unlovely freighters lie in the river, and a few yards off-shore a group of students are sitting decorously over their soft drinks on the deck of a ramshackle floating café called the Kon-Tiki. The atmosphere is breathless: a patina of ancient grime lies over everything, and the Hooghly swirls thickly past us towards the sea, more mud and filth than water. We stand there silently, observing the scene, and as I watch my friend's face I fancy I can identify the various emotions that cross it. There is affection. There is a touch of shame. There is inalienable sadness. There is pride. There is—well, not to put too fine a point upon it, a suggestion of love. It is his country, after all.

He finishes his Cola and takes my bottle from me. "Come on," he gruffly says, "let's go"; and so we get into his shabby old car and hoot our way home, still licking our Choc-O-Luvs, across the fated city.

Boomtown!

HOUSTON, U.S.A.

I have seen *another* future, and for five full days I watched it work! Houston, Texas, is hardly my own idea of a new heaven or a new earth, deposited as it is amorphous and distended up from the sweltering Gulf, but like Lenin's St. Petersburg or Victoria's London, like New York and Chicago in their time, to a large proportion of the human race this improbable metropolis represents the best hope the times can offer.

The world converges upon Houston, Texas. The unemployed pour into town in their hopeful thousands, clutching the Want Ads; the migrants illicit and respectable swell in like a rising tide, talking in unknown tongues; the Icelanders, the Equadorians, the Haitians beaver away in their consulates, the Irish solicit investors to their Industrial Development Authority; the passengers of Andes Airlines, Cayman Island Airways or Sahsa Honduras fly in all agog; the myriad ships tread up the Ship Channel, the scientists beyond number swarm to NASA; hour by hour the freeways get fuller, the downtown towers taller, the River Oaks residents richer, the suburbs gnaw their way deeper into the countryside, and what was just a blob on the map a couple of decades ago becomes more than just a city, but an idea, a vision, the Future Here and Now!

Civic usages elsewhere obsolescent are still in their prime in Houston—boom, burgeon, destiny, dream—and some new words are appositely applied to the city too: *metastasizing,* for instance, which means to spread cancerously and uncontrollably, from cell to cell, from district to district, yesterday the Heights or Tall Timbers, tomorrow desirable addresses or country clubs unborn, far down the freeway where the swamp resumes.

63

But whether the phraseology is toxic or tonic, Houston is one of the few places in the Western world today whose vocabulary is habitually in the future tense, and the positive mood: I will, not I used to, yes rather than sorry, we're out of it. "If you think it's a dump now," a Houstonian said to me with pride, "Wait till you see it in ten years' time. . . ."

—o / o / o—

It is a bit of a dump, I suppose, but of a paradoxical kind. It is the fourth city of the United States, and is changing more spectacularly than any, but still no great city of my experience seems closer to its own roots. So my first day in Houston I spent contemplating the origins of the place.

From the air most of it looks even now like some spasmodic settlement in the scrub, so ubiquitous is its sub-tropical foliage still, and even on the ground the city has decidedly exotic strains. The viscous puddles that lie here and there make me think of mangroves, crocodiles, tsetse flies and things like that, and outside the zoo that first morning, indeed, as I smelt the hot oily breeze off the Gulf, and walked beneath the dark and tangly oaks, and heard the squawks, yaps and wheezes of the creatures inside, I felt myself almost physically transported to a very different city far away—Calcutta of all places, as though the dead men might be lying on the sidewalks of Westheimer, and scabrous lepers haunt Hermann Park.

The solidest layer of the Houston palimpsest, it seemed to me, must be the bottom layer, a sediment of pure Southernness, y'all-ness, bayou-ness, sluggishly defying all the onslaughts of change. The grateful dogwoods, magnolias and loblollys of the suburban streets, the rough buffalo-grass of the parks, the raucous grackles, the humid embrace of the air even in early summer, the dark meandering creeks to be encountered half-buried among the concrete, all made me feel that I was standing in a clearing among the woods. Coyotes, racoons, armadillos naturally, even red wolves I am assured, are still at large within these city limits; egrets, great blue herons, spoonbills are there for the spotting; the hognose snake quite likes the urban life, and even the Houston Toad, described to me in the local manner as The Most Unique Creature in the City, still I was delighted to hear occasionally flops and grunts through Harris County.

The temper of the South is inescapable in Houston. You can see the swagger of it, for example, in the postures of the cattle-people come into town for dinner or convention: hulking rich men in Stetsons and silver belt buckles, paunchy with their generations of beer and prime steaks, lacquered observant women in bangles, talking rather too loud as Texans are apt to, the wives greeting each other with dainty particularities (*"Why, hi Cindy, my you're looking pretty!"*), the husbands with spacious generics (*"Well, boy, what's things like in East Texas?"*).

You can see the poignant charm of it in the faded white clapboard houses of the Fifth Ward, stilted above the dust of their unpaved streets, and conveniently loomed over by the downtown skyscrapers for the benefit of allegorically minded photographers. There the black folk still idle away the warm evenings on their splintered porches, as in the old story books—there the vibrant hymns still rise from the pews of the Rose of Sharon Tabernacle Church—there the garbage still blows about the garden lots, and you may still be asked, as I was, if, say, ain't you Miss Mary's daughter from the old store? "Bless your heart, I used to be one of Miss Mary's best, *best* customers. . . ."

Sometimes too you can taste the old spite and coarseness of the South. Macho rednecks ride ostentatiously around with guns hanging in their pickup cabs; Ku Klux Klansmen threaten the livelihoods of Vietnamese refugees; harsh stories of old southern justice seep in from local jails—chainings, beatings, 148-year sentences, Death Row interviews; just now and then, I fancy, you may detect even in the 1980s a faint spasm of distaste on the faces of the more elderly bellboys in the posh hotels, as they accept the gratuities of their blacker clientele.

But most tellingly of all the southernness of Houston shows in the very place where it all began—Allen's Landing on Buffalo Bayou, where for no very good reason in 1836 the Allen brothers of New York disembarked, pitched their tents in a glade beneath the Spanish moss, and founded the city of Houston. There is no pretending that this historic spot is greatly cherished by Houstonians, most of whom have undoubtedly never set foot there, but lying as it does bang in the middle of town, hardly a stone's throw from the tallest skyscraper west of the Mississippi, just around the corner from the Albert Thomas Convention Center and National Space Hall of Fame, it does startlingly demonstrate how abruptly Houston's future has arrived.

Lord, how it takes one back! Above our heads passes the Main Street viaduct, its pillars scrawled with illiterate graffiti and leant against in the shadows by miscellaneous layabouts. To the west stands the melancholy off-white façade of the Houston Terminal Warehouse Cold Storage. The road behind us forlornly sprouts with grass, like the old roads behind the levees. The trains clank and shunt, as shunt they must in all such southern cameos. And half-hidden down there by its gloomy foliage, tentacled trees and impenetrable brambles, there in the womb of the city slowly swirls the old brown bayou. A ponderous kind of dragonfly frequents this ancient hollow; spin-drift floats about; and when the water momentarily eddies, with a gas bubble perhaps or a Houston Toad, really it might almost be the surfacing of one of those Texan alligators which, in prints of the first steamboat's arrival at this shore, the crew are shown shooting right and left as they churn their passage into history.

$$-o/o/o-$$

But, no, the alligators have probably backed away by now, like the steamboat *Laura M.* itself, which found the Buffalo Bayou too narrow for comfort, and was obliged to retreat from Houston ignominiously stern-first towards the sea. Beside that bayou, upon that swamp, in the succeeding 150 years the Houstonians have built what is in many ways the very model of a modern megapolis, and I spent my second day in the city thinking about *that*. A generation ago this was hick-town, today it possesses all the essentials of American municipal sophistication: to wit, a civically commissioned bronze by Henry Moore, a manic Hyatt Hotel with external elevators, a Gay Quarter (Gay Week in June), a branch of Sotheby's the auctioneers, two or three buildings by Philip Johnson, a symphony orchestra with a Rumanian conductor, a $2 million Picasso in a Fine Arts Museum, restaurants where waiters will sneer at you if you don't want garlic on your shrimps and sidewalk cafés where you may eat healthfood omelettes cooked in bean oil and stuffed with Afghan artichokes.

Houstonians, it dawned upon me that second day, are under the impression that their city is in all respects remarkable. This is because they have seen it grow so explosively from Rice Hotel to Hyatt, visiting stock to City Opera, catfish and hominy grits, I dare say, to *coq au vin* or Afghan artichokes. In fact in most ways it is, to the stranger, rather an unsurprising city. It is much what you expect. The crime rates, police brutalities, traffic congestions and Adult Book Shoppes that Houstonians so deplore are sufficiently familiar to us all; the Hobbit Hole sandwich place has its equivalents, God knows, elsewhere on this planet; the Alley Theatre they never stop talking about is not much different from your repertory company, or mine.

Look at the place as I did, through the traveller's eye. There lies the grid of the old downtown, as it lies everywhere else in America, towered over now of course by the conventional clump of skyscrapers, some plain and ugly by Hankmore, Scribbles, Fujiyama and Olsenjohn Architectural Associates, some slantwise and beautiful by Philip Johnson, all sheathed in those mirrors and tinted windows which make them look, as modern skyscrapers must, utterly unfrequented by sentient beings. There are the usual frenzied ring-roads, upon which citizens here, like citizens everywhere else, earnestly advise you not to venture—Houston's rather bumpier than most, I think, and less intelligently planned than some, but all in all much as you will find them in L.A., Chattanooga, or for that matter Paris, France. There to the west extend the standard interminable suburbs, the rich here, the poor there, the academics in the middle, interrupted occasionally by incipient lesser downtowns and institutions medical sportive or touristical. Houston is perhaps more *splurgy* than its peers because it has done without zoning laws, and it is certainly greener because of that irrepressible foliage; but in its domestic and commercial shape, style and pace it is nothing very special. Astonish me! I like to challenge the cities I visit, but I collected only six items in suburban and downtown Houston, bourgeois Houston that is, which really raised my eyebrows, and here one by one they are:

The labyrinthine downtown tunnel system, so cool, elegant and incomprehensible, which by spewing you calmly into the foyers of totally unexpected office buildings, or the lobbies of hitherto unheard-of hotels, seems to bind the whole place into a mysterious unity.

Jamail's the grocer on Kirby, surely one of the world's supreme supermarkets, where they offer six kinds of English orange marmalade, and where when I went to buy half a pound of cheese to nibble during my explorations it took me a quarter of an hour to narrow my choice down to Irish Blarney or imported Turkish.

The concentrated opulence of River Oaks, even by American standards an unusually well-heeled enclave, but almost comically out of scale with itself—mansion upon mansion, mock-Tudor to Spanish Mission, grand enough to command estates in Virginia or deer-forests in Scotland, but so crammed all together in their poky green yards that there seems hardly space for your five-car garage or your Mexican servants' quarters, let alone room to swing an Abyssinian cat.

The Astrodome in the evening, approached along the South Loop Freeway, when its huge humped dome, set all ablaze by the evening sun, really does look as though it has landed there and then incandescent among its empty parking lot.

The macabre and thrilling mock-up, upstairs in the Albert Thomas Convention Center, of Congressman Thomas's office on Capitol Hill in Washington: nose against the glass I peered with an awful enthralment into this little chamber, and the dim images within, the signed photographs on the walls, the paper knife upon the desk, the foundation-stone hammer, the presentation pens and scrolls, the vaguely perceived portrait of the late Congressman himself upon the wall, made me feel as though I was looking into some unopened dynastic grave, whose treasures would, if I were to shatter the glass in a moment of madness, crumble into dust.

And what else? Surely, you are saying, the famous Galleria? Well, yes, but not its architecture especially, nor the predictably obscene profusion of its merchandise, but something I saw happening upon the ice-rink there, as I sat drinking my coffee on the terrace above. Suddenly the strains of "Yellow Rose of Texas" were gigantically blasted into the glass roof of the arcade; and looking down below me I saw a group of Houston ladies preparing to practice an ice-chorus routine. They struck me, to be frank, as a mature class of chorine, but they swung wonderfully robustly into the gliding steps of their performance—*swing right, one two, swing left, one two, cross over, cross back, into circle one two three*—while all the while the "Yellow Rose" went thump thump from Neiman-Marcus to Lord and Taylor. It was evidently an early stage of their preparations, and just occasionally somebody fell over: but with what dauntless diligence they kept at it, how resolutely they repeated themselves, how indefatigably their leader shrilled her instructions, how untiringly the record player returned, ever and again, to the opening drumbeats of their anthem!

They were your archetypal *doers:* and the true astonishment of Houston, the allure that draws the migrants and fuels the imagination of the nations, is not what it is, still less what it looks like, but what it does.

—o / o / o—

To grasp what it chiefly does, on my third day I went and sat upon a grassy bank beside the Houston Ship Channel, with my back to the old battleship *Texas,* the last of all the world's dreadnoughts, now berthed forever in its dock at San Jacinto Park, and my front to the waterway itself. It is not at all a straightforward waterway, like the Suez Canal, say, since it is really only the same old Buffalo Bayou in disguise, and it winds its way sinuously up from the sea by way of Black Duck Bay and Goat Island, and spills frequently into side-basins and creeks, and is gouged away at the edges into mooring berths. But up and down it night and day the sea-traffic of Houston inexorably proceeds, and I sat in the sunshine there and watched it pass: tankers from Arabia, peculiar Japanese container ships, long strings of blackened barges, queer truncated tugs, ferries, speedboats, sometimes heavy old freighters—ships from sixty nations in 1980, ships from the whole world heading up the old bayou for Houston, Tex.

And the minute they pass the battleship there, with a formal hoot of their sirens sometimes, they enter a stupendous kind of ceremonial avenue, Houston's truest Mall or Champs Elysée: for all up the banks on either side, jagged and interminable stand the oil, chemical and steel plants that have brought Houston into its future—plants with the magical raw names of capitalism, Rohm and Hass, Paktank, Diamond Shamrock, Bethlehem, plants with towers of steel and ominous chimneys, with twisted assemblies of pipes or conduits, with domes, and tanks, and contrapuntal retorts—hissed about here and there by plumes of steam, hung over by vapors, one after the other far away into the haze of the city center, as far as the eye can see towards the distant blurred shape of the skyscrapers.

The Ship Channel takes its vessels almost into the heart of the city, well within the freeway loop. On the western side of town, the suburban side, you would hardly know this staggering complex existed: but it seemed to me down there beside the water as though some irresistible magnetism was impelling those ships willy-nilly upstream into town. Houston is now the first international port of the Western Hemisphere, the place where America's ocean lifeline, as the editorialists like to say, comes ashore at last: that spectacle before me, those ships, that channel, those eerie tanks and towers, really is one of the most significant of all the sights of modern travel.

The power that created Houston also redeems this otherwise banal metropolis. Power must stand in the middle of any Houston essay, for it is power in its most elemental form, the power of physical energy, that has turned this once provincial seaport into a prime force among the

Powers. Houston's publicists like to speak of it as the Giant City, but the truth is far greater than the image, a reversal I think of the Texan norm, and from the indomitable skating ladies of the Galleria to the metallic splendor of the Ship Channel, it was the mighty resolve of the place that moved me most in Houston.

Power pursues power, too, and so the ambition, the opportunity, the greed and the enterprise—the banks and the laboratories, the refiners and the constructors—all coalesce in this city. When the world thinks of Houston, it thinks of bold, brawny, urgent things. If your oil-rig is ablaze in the North Sea or Venezuela, you ring up Red Adair's Oil Well Fires and Blowouts Control Company, out on the Katy Freeway. If your Prime Minister inconveniently collapses in the middle of an election, you send for Dr. Cooley of the Texas Medical Center. If you need a survey of the Hormuz Strait, you get in touch with Western Geophysical Company, 10001 Richmond. And if you want to convey a load of scientific equipment into space, where else to book space on the shuttle but Houston, Tex.?

Actually the most obvious energy down at the NASA Memorial Space Center, when I drove on there that day, seemed to be the enthusiasm of the children who, erupting from endless convoys of buses, burbled, screamed and skidded about the public exhibits preparing class projects, evading the eye of Mrs. Hawkins' Sixth Grade, or perhaps dreaming up the infant poems and aphorisms displayed upon the auditorium walls—

It won't be the life I really new,
It will be the life of the final frontier

or

There once was a ship called Skylab
Skylab was its name
It was launched from Cape Kennedy
And got itself some fame.

The power of the Space Center itself, though, seemed to me of an altogether more steely and calculated kind. It is a distinctly patient power. Some of the astronauts trained here have waited a whole decade before actually going up on a rocket, and now the imagination of the place seems to be groping far, far into the future, far beyond the space shuttles into infinitely distant dreams of the empyrean, with whole cities floating about up there in the dark, and colonies cocooned among the planets, and artificial brightnesses, as they picturesquely say, of A Sun and a Half. The flight control center was empty of people when I was there, but its lights were winking all the same, its digits were faithfully counting down, its great map stood illuminated still between the television screens: it was as though some genius organism was lying low there, counting, thinking, working out the equations before the next colossal effusion of its force.

It is only proper that the very first word ever uttered by a man on the moon should be the name of this city: HOUSTON, radioed Armstrong as soon as he got there, TRANQUILLITY BASE. HERE. THE EAGLE HAS LANDED. As the Mayor of the day was inspired to write, in a composition engraved indelibly on the wall of Tranquillity Park (there are literary advantages to Mayoralty), "the moon has long been humanity's treasure trove . . . so close it could only beckon . . . so far that it could only dare. . . ." As it happens my guide at NASA told me her uncle down at Clear Lake City flatly denies that they ever got to the moon at all, believing it all to be a monumental hoax; but there are many people in Africa, she told me too, who assuming that Houston's association with the heavens has necessarily brought it closer to God himself, write very particularly to this city to order their Bibles.

−o / o / o−

This is undeniably the Big Time. No other city on earth can match this junction of dynamics: no other town is closer to the Almighty! Houstonians at large, though, scarcely seem to notice it. They are hardly modest people, but they are not megapolitan braggers: they do not realize, perhaps, how towering is the reputation of their city—I heard far more about that damned Alley Theatre than ever I did about the ship canal, the petro-chemical industry or manned space flight, and when, pointing out a full moon one night, I ventured to say, "Look, there's Houston's moon up there," my companion failed to notice the allusion, and turned the conversation to a forthcoming performance by the unavoidable Baryshnikov.

On my fourth day in Houston I considered these anomalies. Though newcomers in their hundreds of thousands are invading Houston nowadays, though it is so full of Mexicans already that I sometimes wondered if it could really be called an English-speaking city, though it is in such a state of cosmopolitan flux that my Sierra Leone taxi driver, when I arrived at the airport, invited me to map-read him into town, still your average white middle-class Houstonian seems to honor his city in a distinctly parochial frame of mind. There are strong intimations of the homely in this momentous city. Judge Don E. Walton smokes his pipe as he presides over the 178th District Court down at the County Courthouse, and at one moment I even thought he might put his feet on the table: when I inadvertently found myself included in jury selection, I was touched how elementary, how childlike almost, was the exposition of the Common Law thought necessary for the miscellaneous housewives, wispy pensioners, sagging businessmen and bewildered Hispanics about to decide the fate of the poor devil under trial. Wow! is the habitual response of Houstonians, I discovered by hanging around his cage, to the Binturog who is a prime exhibit of their zoo: and on the whole Wow!, no less, no more, seems to enunciate their response to their city's new-found greatness.

Three million strong already, the energy capital of the Western world, Moon-City, The Giant, still Houston looks back affectionately to its homegrown heroes and backyard epics. This is an agreeable trait, but it makes for myths and iconographies baffling to the uninstructed visitor. The eponymous Sam Houston, a hero otherwise unsung in the larger world, rides still, cloak a-flying, through Houston's civic consciousness. The glories of San Jacinto, the tragic memories of Goliad, recur all too obscurely in municipal pamphlets. What was this Rice, for whom an entire university is named? Who were these Hobbys, immortalized in an airport? What knight of the bayous, what swash-buckler of the swamp, gave his name to Blodgett Street?

Houston is a tight town, I think. It has its raffish parts of course, its fair share of the contemporary violence, its streak of the insensitivity which is part of the southern heritage. But its general posture strikes me as respectable and conventional. Even Montrose, the quarter of town most hospitable to quirks and exceptions, is remarkably genteel of mien; even at Butera's, a hangout frequented by writers, artists and the like, hard though I tried I could find no outrageous exhibitionists. The 1960s were so long ago by Houston's calendar that they seem never to have happened in this city at all, and I find it hard indeed to imagine draft cards burnt upon the trim Rice campus, or hear the rhythms of Baez or Dylan dirge-like over Memorial Park. Jews tell me they sometimes sense loveless vibes

in Houston, and for myself, as an anti-nuclear neutralist, animal liberationist, Welsh nationalist and aspirant anarchist, I am seldom altogether
at ease with the stern Free World exhortations of the Houston *Post* or
Chronicle.

It feels a city, too, of strong and close alliances, bonds of neighborhood,
profession or background, whose direct loyalties are to Bellaire, say, the
Symphony League, the principle of vascular stimulation in cardiac ther-
apy, or most of all perhaps to your own resilient family. There are five
columns of Rices in the Houston telephone book, three of Houstons, and
fourteen lines of Blodgetts: and when I went to a gallery party one evening in town, I found that not only did all the other guests seem to be
related to the well-known local artist we were honoring, but the shop
itself belonged to his mother-in-law—"you must be from out of town,"
said one eminent old body indulgently when I expressed surprise at these
happy arrangements.

I missed some element of salt or spice to flavor this somewhat steak-like
city. I pined for fantasy in Houston, Texas! I was sitting that same evening in a house in—well, in Sherwood Acres let us say, for I do not wish
to be discourteous, engaged in a characteristically Sherwood Acres con-
versation, not altogether unrelated to the Alley Theatre and the Rumanian conductor, when I looked through the window and saw a dream-
like figure pass sauntering by. He had a sack over his arm, and a stick
over his shoulder, and he wore a high-crowned hat and a cloak I think,
and his face was black and bearded, and he strolled past easy, insolent
and amused. On my fourth day in Houston, my heart leapt to see him.
"Who was that?" I cried, rushing to the window, "that man with the
stick, and the high-crowned hat, and the sack on his arm?" But there
was no one there, and my hostess returned me a little reprovingly to our
discussion. "I saw nobody," she sweetly and carefully said. "But tell me,
have you had time to see our new Picasso in the Fine Arts Museum?
And will you have an opportunity to meet with Mrs. Oveta Culp
Hobby?"

—o / o / o—

And so on my fifth day in Houston I tried to imagine the future of
this Future. Actually I went to have my palm read by Mrs. Williams, on
Holcombe Boulevard—you know, just around the corner from the Tot
Haven Progressive Child Day Center. She charged me five bucks, shoo'd

away the children and prophesied that with God's help I would presently overcome my jealous enemies and move to Houston myself. "You will not like it at first," said Mrs. Williams, eyeing me rather shrewdly I thought, "but with God's help you will get used to it."

Well, maybe. The centripetal quality of Houston is undeniable, and nobody can be altogether immune to the blazing promise of the place. Who in an impoverished world can look unmoved upon forty Sunday pages of Help Wanted, for architects as for rig drillers, blasting supervisors and dental ceramists, restaurant managers for Burger King or polygraph examiners for Image Research Inc.? And who in a jaded world, sapped by nostalgia, disheartened by experience, can be left unexcited by a city that looks so confidently and ruthlessly ahead? In seventy-five years, they say, Houston may well achieve the grandest and brashest of all its ambitions, to be the ultimate city of them all, the greatest conglomeration of energies and artifacts ever known to history. Now who can sneer at *that?*

But then the future never lasts. "Sir," said the train conductor to Charles Dickens the novelist, as they ran into Chicago a century ago. "Sir, you are entering the Boss City of the Universe." Today it is Houston that greets its settlers and visitors with such grand hyperbole, but its particular future is doubtless just as ephemeral as any other. Look at Leningrad! Look at London! Look at knocked-about New York! In fact I felt to this city something especially transient and impermanent: I could not see it getting old—it doesn't feel built to last—and on my last day in town a dark and fateful fancy overcame me, and I seemed to see the City of Destiny abandoning itself after all, the whole grand circus of it moving out again, and in an exodus as terrific as its influx, pouring away once more down the waterways and freeways.

I saw in my mind's eye the Mexicans streaming for the border, their cars hung all about with beds, baskets and bundles—I saw the oil men hastening out from Hobby in their Gulfstreams and helicopters—the smoke of burning documents from the roofs of consulates—the Amtrak for the North bursting with fugitives, wistfully looking through its sealed windows for a last glimpse of dear old Sherwood Acres—the last ship swinging in the turning basin, to sail away past the deserted *Texas* to the open sea—the final flight of Cayman Island Airways announcing its departure to the East—the terminal patients at the Texas Medical Center passed tenderly, entangled with tubes and drippers, into their waiting ambulances—the last pipe closed, the last tank emptied, the last furnace dampened at Exxon or Armco Steel—the last shuttle controllers switching off, with a sigh, those blinking lights and digitals down at the Space Center.

And then, gleaming but sterile in the sunshine, crinkle-reflected still in each others' mirror-glass, I saw the empty downtown skyscrapers left like tombs, all elevators stilled, as memorials to the future past: while the cottonwood, the hickory and the Spanish moss, creeping up again from the bayou, entangled parks and gardens once again, choked the downtown tunnels, and wormed a way into all the fancy plazas.

Not So Far

A EUROPEAN JOURNEY

The farm dog leapt from the gate and snapped enthusiastically at my hub caps. Somebody waved goodbye, teacup in hand, from the Parrys' front window. I met the postman in his van halfway up the lane, and through his window he passed me an electricity bill, a notice about next week's bring-and-buy sale at the village hall, and three chances to win £50,000 in a Reader's Digest Prize Draw. There was snow on the high summit of Moel Hebog, the hefty bald mountain in front of me; behind my back the Irish Sea lay silent beneath a cold and western sheen.

I was leaving on a European journey: from this far Welsh corner of the continent, looking across to Ireland, to Montenegro on the other side of it, looking down to Albania. I was about to cross, not just a geographical conglomeration, or a historical expression, but a civilization: between these two extremes some 200 million people, whether they admit it or not, live to a common heritage and a more or less common set of values. This is the ghost of the Roman Empire, still perceptible after so many centuries of exorcism: if the Irish in the West never were subject to the Roman order, and have consequentially lived in tumultuous distemper ever since, the Albanians in the East have long disowned the patrimony, and live in a state of chill and utter isolation, the only people on earth among whom all forms of religion are strictly prohibited.

The rest of us along the route, Welsh, English, French, Italian, Swiss, Yugoslavs, are members really, for all our political styles, of the same spectral commonwealth. The great motorways which now criss-cross all

Europe are only late successors to the high roads of the legions. The gradual weakening of nationality in western Europe, the blurring of frontiers, the mixing of languages, even the universal acceptance of bank and credit cards, which means I could really travel from Caernarfon to Cetinje without a solid penny in my pocket—all these phenomena of the 1980s are only returns to the imperial conveniences of Rome.

So I hardly felt I was going abroad, when I hit the main Dolgellau road and headed for England and the southeast: for most Europeans nowadays abroad is somewhere else altogether—east of Suez, say, south of the Equator, Ireland or Albania. "Going far, then?" inquired the garage-man, when I stopped to fill up. "Montenegro," I said, but he was not in the least surprised. "Oh yes," he said. "The wife and I had a nice little holiday at Petrovac a year or two back. Check your oil, shall I?"

–o / o / o–

It is as though the British Isles are tilted permanently to one corner— the southeast corner, bottom right, where London stands seething upon the Thames. Everything slithers and tumbles down there, all the talent, all the money, and when I got on to the M4 motorway that morning I felt that I was being swept away helter-skelter, willy-nilly across the breadth of England. Around me all the energies of the place seemed to be heading in a single direction—the trucks from Cornwall and South Wales, the tourist buses, the ramshackle No Nuclear estate cars, the stream of expense-account Fords, their salesmen drivers tapping their steering-wheels to the rhythm of Radio One. London! London! shouted the direction signs. London! screamed the blue and white train, streaking eastwards beside the road, and when I turned off to the south and made for Dover, still I felt the presence of the capital tugging away at me, as it tugs the commuters from their mock-Tudor villas day after day from the far reaches of Surrey and pastoral Hampshire.

Mrs. Thatcher's Britain is an uneasy kingdom, a kingdom of anomalies. It is poor but it is rich. It is weak but it is resilient. It is very clever in some ways, thick as mutton in others. It wins more Nobel Prizes per capita than any other nation, yet it can hardly keep its head above bankruptcy. It is socially at loggerheads with itself, but is united in a sentimental passion for the charade of monarchy. Even the sensations of a motorway drive like ours are muddled and puzzling, as we pass out of the poor wild mountains of Wales, where there are far more sheep than humans, so swiftly into the most thickly populated and intensely developed landscape in Europe. The road is bumpy and often interrupted by desultory road works, there being not enough money to maintain it properly: yet beside it the lovely manor houses stand serene as ever in their old walled gardens, the villages cluster cosily around, the cows are plump, the meadowlands green and rich. The mid-day radio news speaks of more education cuts, rising unemployment, falling production, protest marches, civil servants' strikes: but all around us the cars of the indigent British, most of them imported, hasten eastwards at the statutory 70 m.p.h. on gasoline at £1.81 a gallon.

And the queerest anomaly of all is the condition of the southeast, the flatlands in fief to London, for there all the middle-class values, surviving everything that socialism has tried to do to them, complacently flourish through crisis and decline. By afternoon I was entering that cosy never-never land, and it was like entering an imaginary England, in an old movie or a rather dated novel. Glossy and mullion-windowed stood the commuter houses behind their privet hedges and ornamental gates, and there were boats on trailers beside their garages, and horse-boxes often, and girls in jodhpurs trundled about on ponies, talking in such well-enunciated voices that I could hear, or at least vividly imagine, snatches of their conversations through my open roof—"Absolutely super food . . ." "He's an absolute twit . . ." or "God, Jennifer, I do believe this bloody muffle's breaking again. . . ."

Ample dormitory-towns stood all along my route, Haslemere and Guildford, Dorking and Leatherhead: ageless comfortable towns, medieval merged with modern, chain supermarket beside old family grocer, Sew-'n'-Knit or Pots & Things cheek by jowl with Edward H. Rigby, Ironmongers since 1767—smug, fancy little towns with bulging car-parks and gilded municipal clocks, with pleasure-boats lined up for hire on willow-shaded streams, with well-built women wearing headscarves and pushing shopping-baskets on wheels, with Olde Englyshe Tea Rooms and grand half-timbered coaching-inns advertising Real Ales and Scampi-in-the-Basket.

No slums, no rotting factories, no lines of bitter unemployed. This is true Thatcher country. The rotten teeth of Britain are elsewhere—here are only the satisfied digestive juices. You will hear no raw or earthy dialects down here: this is the home of standard English, BBC English, and the accents of the countryside have long since been poshed up or homogenized—even the countryside itself, indeed, for though there are patches of fine green farmland between the towns, it never breaks away altogether from the urban pull, but is like some intermittent park or genteel garden, worked perhaps by business people as a week-end recreation.

It is a pleasant and fortunate country, but it never chills the spine or raises the heart. It is Lotus Land Class Two. But by tea-time anyway I had broken away from it into the open Kentish grasslands, and before it was dark I was running down the cliffside road to Dover beneath its glowering castle, a town all bashed about by wars and history, a town without illusions, not a Lotus-town at all, which inspects my passport with a sneer and shoves me unceremoniously, as if glad to get rid of me, on board a boat for France.

$$-o\,/\,o\,/\,o-$$

A boat for France! There is always a boat for France. Night and day for a thousand years or more, if you turn up at Dover you will find a boat for France. The English Channel here is the busiest waterway on earth, and in the high summer season there is a car-ferry out of Dover every ten minutes. Whenever I looked out of the *Free Enterprise*'s windows, as dusk fell over the sea, somewhere out there another ferry was stubbing its bows into the swell: and once I saw, a weird black shape half-hidden by flying spray, the whirring scudding passage of a hovercraft in the grey.

The car was clamped below decks, towered over by the mighty juggernaut trucks, German, Dutch, French, British, Italian, even Bulgarian or Rumanian, which are the colorful familiars of modern Europe. Upstairs the ship had apparently been hijacked by demoniac schoolchildren. They clustered in mobs around the Space Invaders machine. They stormed the souvenir shop. They experimented with foreign currencies in the coffee machine. They tripped up passing stewards. They shouted hilarious insults at each other. They lurched in screaming phalanxes up and down stairs.

Some were British, some French, some Italian, some Finnish for all I know, but physically they were indistinguishable. As we approached the French coast they were marshalled into some sort of discipline by pimply bearded schoolteachers, and I left them standing there waiting for the gangplank to go down in a condition of sullen suppression, interspersed now and then with giggles and belches. Their teachers surveyed them with distaste. A few elderly tourists stood warily around their flanks. The ship docked with a bit of a bump, and faintly above the roar of the starting engines, from far below on the car deck, I heard their eldritch shrieks.

–o / o / o–

Years ago the scholar D. W. Brogan warned us that we were about to see a new marvel: a young France, which had not existed since the nineteenth century, before the double decimation of the two World Wars. Well, now we have it, and among all the countries of western Europe, none has changed so fast or so dramatically as France.

The French police did not bother to inspect my passport, as I drove ashore at Calais. They are not in the mood for trivia these days. If individually the French are as pesky, as charming, as irreverent, as bloody-minded, as profoundly conservative as ever, corporately they have become forceful and rather flashy. The momentum of Autoroute N1 towards Paris is twice as powerful as the movement of the M4 towards London, and this is not only because the speed limit is higher, but because the drivers are more demanding, more exhibitionist and more opportunist, and because Paris is not just the capital of a State but the true hub of the Continent. If the energies of Britain slide down to London as though the country is tilted that way, the traffic from Belgium, Germany, Holland, Sweden even, presses down the Autoroute towards Paris with an eager expectancy.

Everything seems to be brand new on this steely thoroughfare. The road itself is newish, a product of France's "Economic Miracle," the cars are new, the signs are new, and every town we pass is clumped about by brand-new concrete blocks, relentlessly French and functional. When I stop for a cup of coffee, all in the café is automated: the coffee churns from electronic urns, the rolls and croissants are stacked in their identical thousands, all is wink of control light and bleep of computerized till. France is young again. The middle-aged truck-driver standing beside me at the plastic-covered chairless table munches his hamburger with a far-away look, gazing out through the automatic doors as if he sees out there, away beyond the Autoroute, dim visions of soup tureens, checked tablecloths and bombazine.

He is going to have to live, though, with the plastic table and the hamburger. They are the penalties of new youth. Instant food, nuclear power, missile submarines, the anglicization of the French language—all these are part of the ambience of Young France, an ironic factor in that national greatness without which, De Gaulle, the supreme traditionalist once said, France would never truly be France. And yet, and yet. . . .

By nightfall I was in Burgundy, eating snails, drinking Sauvignon de Saint-Bries, and after dinner I walked out through the village to sniff the night air. The long main street was quiet and empty. Only occasionally did a truck roar through to Dijon, or a car spring away with a showy blare of exhausts from the Café des Voyageurs beside the crossroads. Chained dogs barked, one after the other as I passed, from behind high iron gates. Impertinently peering through window-chinks, I caught glimpses of polished brass, ornamental clocks, lace cushion-covers, lines of washing stretched beside fireplaces, all illuminated by the flickering multicolored lights of the TV sets—over which, in every house, dim shawled and coated figures seemed to be silently crouching, very close to the screen. Though as I approached the café I could hear the cheerful sounds of rock, and though there were five or six Yamahas and Suzukis outside it, and a red Renault Turbo, still as I walked up the street beneath the pollarded limes I felt the old France still stirring all around me, embodied above all not in the sights, nor the sounds, nor the texture of the night, but in the smells.

Only slightly intoxicated by the wine, only minimally slowed down by the snails, only occasionally interrupted in my thought—*swoosh!*—by the passing of a truck, as I wandered up the street I identified those old fragrances one by one in my mind. There was the old masonry and woodwork of the village itself, of course. There was hay, and dung to go with it. There was the smell of mossy water, from the old fountain with the lion's head beside the bridge. There was that faint smell of good cooking which, even in the age of convenience foods, still hangs habitually about French homesteads. There was a hint of some evening blossom, lime perhaps, or honeysuckle. There was an emanation of wood fires, and a distinct soupçon of dry rot, and a hint of coffee, and something vinous or brandeine or Chartreusian underlying it all.

At the top of the street I found that the parish church had a large square porch jutting into the street, so I stepped inside, and from its shadows looked back through the trees down the length of the village.

Inside that structure, I discovered, all the smells were permanently concentrated, jammed together in a sort of solid essence between the old
pillars: food, dog, dung, hay, damp, stone, rot, blossom, fire and lichened
water all in one. And so I leant against the wall there for a few minutes,
relishing this heady elixir, watching the comings and going from the
Café des Voyageurs, whose lights spilt out across the village street, and
whose juke-box beat with a lively thump through the barking of the dogs.

–o / o / o–

The frontier between France and Switzerland, in the outskirts of Geneva,
is almost indistinguishable among the suburbs, but it is a special kind of
frontier all the same. It is the frontier of detachment. It marks the line
between a nation repeatedly ravaged, humiliated and ennobled by war,
and a nation which has for generations resolutely, almost contemptuously
stood aside from the internecine squabbles of Europe—between the grand
epitome of the nations, in whose destinies we all seem to share, and a
nation which holds itself aloof to the comradeships of pride and suffering.
Even today Switzerland is a State apart, an enclave within the Europe
of which it forms an essential crossroads, a member of no alliance, an
adherent of no bloc, where unemployment scarcely exists, everyone is
middle class, and the rich of all nations come to live in bland tax-free
alpine villas among the flowers, snows and numbered bank accounts.

Something has gone wrong, though, in this milky paradise. I remember writing, not so long ago, that if ever I felt relieved to cross the border
from France into Switzerland, I would know I was getting old—I would
have come to prefer serenity to stimulation, calm to excitement. No such
denouement threatens now. Switzerland has lost its plush and easy motion, and Geneva, once so sure and dull, now seems above all restless, as
though it is unsure of its own identity, and after all these years of complacency, is having second thoughts. It suggests to me one huge airport
lounge, sleepless, dissatisfied, inhabited by world-weary duty-free conces-
sionaires and slightly jet-lagged transients, coming and going night and
day in a time-zone haze beside the lovely lake.

–o / o / o–

The lake is always lovely. At night it is resplendent with its parade of
neon signs, red and green and blue and yellow on buildings all around,
stacked winking and blinking above the water against the misty back-

ground of the mountains. In the daylight it is spectacular with the great plume of its fountain, spouting a couple of hundred feet into the air above the harbor mole, and with the graceful movements of its boats, the veteran launches which potter back and forth from one city quarter to another, the elegant old steamers which, bow-spritted and slant-funnelled, sail swan-like away in the morning mist for their beloved circuits of the lake.

But if the setting is still celestial—if the air is clear and clean—if the clouds sometimes part in the east to reveal the magnificence of Mont Blanc itself, attended by all its pinnacles—nevertheless there is a niggling, prodding sense of unease in the air of Geneva nowadays. "Shall we have a quiet week-end?" asked the *Tribune de Genève* nervously the day I arrived: for though they have not yet had youth riots here (as they have repeatedly in Zurich up the road), still there is an abrasive kind of fizz to the city now, harsh and humorless.

I lunched with a spy of my acquaintance. What kind of a spy he is, who he spies for, or against, I have never been able to discover; but he has all the hallmarks of espionage about him, divides his time between Switzerland and the East, wears raincoats and speaks Greek. We ate little grilled fish at the water's edge, as we generally do when I am passing through Geneva, and discussed the state of the city. Uncomfortable, he thought it, and getting more so. Security getting tougher, I surmised? Banks turning difficult? Opposition hotter? No, no, no, he said testily, nothing like that: only those damned roller-skaters.

Roller-skating is all the rage around the Lake of Geneva. Whole families skate along the promenade. Dogs ride about in rollered baskets, and youths whizz shatteringly here and there, scattering the crowds before them with blasts of the whistles that are held between their teeth. "Dear God, those whistles," said the spy, holding his hands over his ears, and indeed those harsh blasts struck me as a *leit-motif* or perhaps a *cri-de-coeur* of contemporary Geneva, at once aggressive and despairing, cynical and abusive. When after lunch that Sunday afternoon I wandered around the lake to watch the world go by I found that everything I saw, everything I heard down there, was punctuated by the shrill passage of the roller-skaters.

In particular I see their hurtling forms in my mind's eye when I recall a revivalist meeting I found in progress not far from the Pont du Mont Blanc, where the footpath curves around beneath the trees towards the eastern shore of the lake. This was a pathetic spectacle. A young man in a neat grey suit was preaching repentance on the sidewalk, backed by four earnest helpers with guitars, and around them there had assembled a characteristic Geneva Sunday crowd—people of every color, every kind, black people, gowned Arabs, Chinese, a flamboyant covey of Nigerians, three mountain people like Sherpas or Bhutanis, one or two half-hearted local hecklers, half-a-dozen of those middle-aged, middle-class middling sort of men, widowers I expect, to be seen in any park of the Western world wandering aimlessly about on Sunday afternoons.

It was a very subdued brand of fundamentalism that those zealots were offering, there in the city of Calvin himself. The preacher's voice was gentle, the guitars were muted, when they broke into a hymn it was remorseful rather than rousing, and even the hecklers hardly raised their voices. Behind them the lake shone happily, all flags, masts and fountain, and ever and again a dear old Edwardian motor-launch, so overloaded in the stern that her cantonal flag sometimes trailed in the water, cruised from shore to shore like a prop on a circular stage.

The preacher preached, the hecklers mildly scoffed, the guitarists strummed, the motley crowd watched all in silence—and through them in brutal counterpoint hurtled the roller-skaters of Geneva, behind them, before them, between the preacher and his audience, between the guitarists and me, heads down, whistles blowing, on their faces expressions not of fun, humor, fellowship or human sympathy, but of cheerless and unremitting arrogance.

–o / o / o–

High in the rockface above Chamonix, a huddle of brownish structures, a mesh of steel girdering, a great hole in the mountainside—the Mont Blanc Tunnel. The road winds heavily out of the Chamonix valley to reach it, and the effect is Wagnerian. The white massif looms operatically high above; the great trucks lumber around the horseshoe bends like so many giants; what dread enchantment, you may wonder, dwells within that hole, what fancy of Grimm or Tolkien, what Worm of the Alps?

They tell me that when the tunnel was first opened migrating swallows used it to save themselves a flight over the mountains: and for people of the cold north, like me, it offers an almost symbolic transference to the warm south of our profoundest desires. No birds could fly through it now, for it is a tube heavy always with fumes and chemicals, but still as I climbed up to it that day I felt a bit like a swallow myself, genetically impelled towards the sun. The valley behind me, playing up to the allegory, was thick with grey mist, and the peaks above swirled with cloud: but at the other end of that noxious worm-hole, surely the sparkle awaited me.

And so, magically, it proved. The bare dank rock of the tunnel swept by me in the darkness, the illuminated signs kilometer by kilometer, the little sheltering alcoves with the emergency telephones, and presently far in the distance I saw a tiny circle of bright yellow light, hardly bigger than a pinhead. Like a bird I pursued it, and larger it grew, and brighter, and yellower, and presently it lost its outline, and came flooding into the tunnel to greet me, and dazzled me with its splendor—and it was the sunshine of Italy, on the warm side of the Alps!

I was there where the beakers brimmed. I had crossed the watershed of Europe, and had passed from the grey to the gold. Within the hour I was drifting poetically about on Lake Viverone, drinking martinis and observing the courting displays of the ever-lusty crested grebe.

$$-o\,/\,o\,/\,o-$$

There used to be four golden stallions, loot from old Byzantium, gloriously above the great central doorway of the Basilica San Marco in Venice. For 800 years they stood there as the supreme symbol of Venetian independence and stability. When I walked into the Piazza San Marco, though, I found only one beast up there on the gallery, and he was hardly golden, but rather a sort of brown dunnish color, and he had none of the scars and wrinkles of age upon him, none of the dents and roughenings, but seemed to stand there altogether too perfectly, too trim, neat and self-conscious.

What did I expect? demanded the man selling postcards beside the flagpoles below. That horse was a sham. The real ones had been removed to a museum chamber out of sight, and they are to be replaced in the end by four such copies: meticulous copies, lovingly made, exactly proportioned, but inevitably lacking the mysterious fire of genius, antiquity, or divinity. I asked the postcard man what he thought about it, and he said it was progress, that's all, progress, you couldn't stop it. But to my mind the appearance of the first of these poor substitutes upon that belvedere marks a fundamental turning point in the fortunes of Venice. At last pretense has definitively taken over from reality. The ancient metropolis, for more than a thousand years one of the Powers of Europe, has

abandoned the long effort to maintain itself as a real working city, and
accepted its status as an exhibition place, a holiday town, a conference
center, where perfect sham horses make more sense than knocked-about
old real ones, and age itself is something to be honored in guide books
and scholarly theses, but disguised or circumvented in life.

It is a relief for me. I have been protesting too long, hoping always that
Venice would somehow recover its ancient greatness as a great mercantile
or financial entrepôt, a channel between East and West, dreading the moment when it would be no more than a museum, petulantly scoffing at
its restoration and from time to time declaring the wish that it would
sink. Now, quite suddenly, I can scoff and argue no more. Venice has
abandoned the old fight, thrown off the nostalgia and the melancholy,
and is proceeding with gusto into the ordinary world. It has not been so
lively since the fall of the Venetian Republic, nearly 200 years ago.

Often in the evenings I wandered, like everyone else, around the arcades
of the Piazza, Napoleon's finest drawing-room in Europe, and wondered
at the vivid, boisterous, almost violent new spirit of the place. The café
orchestras string away still of course, at "Rose Marie," "Oklahoma," or a
contemporary favorite of theirs, "It's Up to You, New York, New York."
But they are rivalled nowadays by other sorts of music: transistor music
from groups of students huddled upon the steps of the arcades, or cross-
legged in circles upon the paving-stones; country music perhaps from a
boy with a guitar at the foot of the campanile, with a huge crowd singing
and swaying with him in the half-light; snatches of song from hilarious
Italian school-children, snatches of trumpet one evening from a man lurching tipsily round the corner of the Doge's Palace wearing a cocked hat
and riding-breeches, snatches of cheerful whistle from me, for I rather
enjoyed this vigorous new cacophony, and thought if you couldn't have
the Four Stallions of St. Mark, you could do worse than turn the Piazza
into a kind of disco.

It is not, though, just in the show of it that Venice has changed in the
last year or two. More and more it is becoming a city of rich retreat, where
tycoons of Turin or Milan may spend secure and sybaritic week-ends,
where pop stars and millionaires from all Europe may live it up with
wild parties in romantic palaces. The Venetian working people are being
forced out of the city, all too often, by rising prices, to turn themselves
into mainlanders over the causeway in Mestre, where they may look
back to the towers of their ancestral home with mingled relief and long-

ing. The little neighborhood shops are disappearing one by one. Carnival has returned to Venice, and for two weeks in Lent the city bursts into a communal festivity which may well again become, so social experts assure me, one of the great events of the European calendar.

"Progress, that's all. . . ." Only here and there in the islands of the Venetian lagoon, still when the weather is right shrouded in a mysterious suggestiveness, are there pockets of resistance to the Newing of Venice. Not everybody wants the lagoon jazzed up with casinos, tourist complexes, love-nests or, as is seriously proposed for one island, "Caribbean-style Beach Complexes." I was told that on the island of Santa Fessola, for instance, two monks of the Dominican Order had dug themselves in to resist all change: so I hired a motorboat at once and sailed out there to meet them.

Until recently Santa Fessola was an isolation hospital, and all its buildings still stand, slowly crumbling, half-overgrown by prickly creepers and flicked about by lizards. At first when I disembarked upon this desolate shore I could find no sign of human life: only the dry grass crackled beneath my feet, and the old doors, sagging upon their rusty hinges, creaked theatrically when I pushed them. Just when I was about to give up, though, I heard a shout, and there were the two protestors, emerging from some hidden recess of the hospital and hastening down to the water-stage towards me. One was young and plump, the other old and white-bearded, and a little black dog scampered around them. They were cheerful men, but implacable. There among the toppling ruins they would stay, they said, come what may, to ensure that nothing dreadful happened to the island. Had they any notion what might happen to it? They raised their hands and eyes to heaven: anything might happen, they said, as though the Black Angel himself might be planning to develop the place.

Though the sun shone brightly and the breeze was warm, theirs seemed a melancholy dedication, so lonely the island, so decrepit those buildings, so far away the light and life of Venice. When I sailed away again, and looked back to the ugly white structures among the landing-stage, their plaster peeling and their roofs beginning to topple, in a round oriel window on the first floor I saw the weathered, wistful but still rosy face of the old brother, exactly framed in the window, as in a Renaissance portrait. He was looking fixedly out at me: when I waved he raised his hand in a tentative way, and from far out in the lagoon I could still discern his presence there, peering motionless through that window.

–o / o / o –

In the bare desiccated hills above Trieste stands the Yugoslav frontier post. I could see its lights up the road there, but it took me a good hour to reach them. Backed far down the highway to the city were the lines of Yugoslavs waiting to get home after the week-end. They had been to the great street market of Trieste, most of them, to stock up with jeans, radios, coffee or perhaps gold; they had brought their children and mothers-in-law for the ride; now they sat there, engines throbbing, sometimes lurching a few feet forward, sometimes getting out of the car to stretch their arms, waiting helplessly in the gathering darkness to get home again to the Peoples' Republic. The hills were dark and empty all around us: when I looked behind I could see the lights of the waiting cars fender to fender all down the hill towards the sea.

The Yugoslavs were used to it. It is always like this. Halfway up the hill somebody had set up a mobile canteen, and they were selling coffee and hamburgers from the back of a truck. Occasionally some know-all, scudding up beside us on the gravel, plunged on to a dirt track up the side of the mountain, never to be seen again. Once a pair of gigantic trucks, from Mostar, the old Turkish town in Herzogovina, forced their way by sheer bulk and judder yard by yard up the waiting queue, blocking all other movement until, with a hissing of air-brakes and roar of engines, they disappeared triumphantly over the crest of the hill.

At last I reached the frontier post. The lights were dim. An official with a red star on his cap beckoned for my passport without a word and slowly examined every page. Without a smile, without a flicker, with only a gloomy stare he handed it back to me.

"Cheer up," I said.

"Enjoy yourself," he morosely replied, and waved me into the dusk.

–o / o / o –

Ah well, Yugoslavia is like that. It hardly offers a laughing welcome to its guests, but there is scarcely a soul in the country who will not respond to a little jollying along, and whose native surliness cannot be softened, given time and practice, into bonhomie. I drove down the grand Adriatic Highway, winding between the high limestone escarpment and the island-speckled sea, in a state of elation, playing Mozart all the way, stopping now and then for grilled fish and prosek, inspecting a church here, a castle there, until I reached the old port of Split, Spalato to the Italians, and there settled down for a few days doing nothing on the waterfront.

I always feel happy on the Dalmatian coast of Yugoslavia. It suits me. I like its mean between simplicity and sophistication, between communism and capitalism, between the local and the national. I like to go into a supermarket and find it moderately, temperately stocked, without that vulgar profusion of choice which makes the modern Western store seem a little obscene to the traveller, without the boorish austerity of your whole-hog Soviet Grocer No. 4. I like the sense of wry comradeship which, with an almost universal flashing of lights and comical gestures, warns you that there is a speed trap down the road. I like the ships which are always in sight, fishing boats loitering among the green islets, tall white ferry-steamers chugging into port, tankers in dry docks up unexpected creeks, motor torpedo-boats in gray clusters at their moorings, hydrofoils flashing off for Venice—ships always and everywhere along that incomparable coast, pervading every image and crossing every vista.

It is the sexiest of coasts, the most virile, the lustiest. Bold are its men, brave its women, doggedly its children hold back their tears; Tito would be proud of them still. I drove out from Split one day to buy a bottle of black wine from a country homestead, and wonderfully earthy and organic was the domestic hierarchy I discovered inside the house: a brawny stubbly farmer-husband, a tough buxom wife, a one-eyed cat, a sprightly terrier, and in a steamy scullery behind the kitchen, the Wine-Mother herself in the fullness of her years, stirring and tasting and stirring again—"Good health, good luck," cried these amiable bucolics as they filled my glass, and bonk, when I returned to the car I tripped on a stick, and went back to town dripping thick black country wine all over the bonnet, as though I had been baptized by gods of revelry.

Not that Split is exactly a frivolous place, any more than Yugoslavia is a frivolous kind of country. The city is built around the old imperial palace of Diocletian, a Split-born Roman Emperor, whose walls still form the outlines of the inner town, and this gives it a mighty imperial stance, with its wide harbor in front, its new concrete suburbs stretching away in heavy clusters to the hills behind. It is a city of terrific innuendo. Its citizens are magnificently stalwart—Split people must be the tallest in Europe, if not in the world—and the place hums with a sort of suppressed dynamism, as if it is always about to break into. . . .

Well, into what? Probably into nothing at all. All Europe is seized with a restlessness these days. It is muffled by prosperity and restrained by the Welfare State in its various guises—as Bismarck once observed, nothing maintains the status quo better than social security for all. In Yugoslavia, though, it is nearer the surface than it is in—well, in Dorking, say. The Yugoslavs are a people accustomed to living dangerously. In war they fought with insatiable savagery, in peace they have walked a political tightrope. They seem to me to be bursting with an energy only just controllable, like steam in a boiler.

Perhaps it is a consequence of their system—not quite tyrannical, not quite free. Perhaps it is a heritage of Balkanism, that fissiparous, conspiratorial instinct which kept this corner of Europe for so many generations in conflict and uncertainty. Or perhaps it is just the natural temperament of the people—Slavs of the Mediterranean, through whose history the warm and the cold winds paradoxically buffet, and in whose spirit the grim and the jolly seem so curiously allied.

Split is a naval base, and when I was driving out of town at the end of my stay I stopped at a traffic light near the fleet headquarters. A very senior Yugoslav naval officer started to cross the road. He was loaded with badges, braid and medal ribbons; but wearing as I was a floppy old canvas hat and a less than spotless blue shirt, just for fun I saluted him. His response was Split all over. First he faltered slightly in his steady tread. Then he brought his hand to the peak of his cap in a guarded and cautious way. And then, as the lights changed, I started forward, and he scuttled with rather less than an admiral's dignity to the safety of the opposite sidewalk, he turned around, all rank and propriety discarded, and shared my childish laughter.

–o / o / o –

"Back again," said the magnifico at the café on the road into the Black Mountains, on the last ridge before Cetinje and the heart of Montenegro. We had met before, you see. He is always there, it seems, summer or winter, like a major-domo of these uplands, or a Chief of Protocol. He wears black breeches, and a wide belt like a cummerbund, and he stands about seven feet tall, and speaks in a basso profondo, and tosses slivovic back like lime juice, and is in fact in all respects the very model of a modern Montenegrin.

With this splendid fellow at my side, kneading his moustaches, I sat

down on the bench outside the café, and looked back, far down the cork-
screw Kotor road, far up the glittering Dalmatian coast, along the way I
had come. I had journeyed from one extremity to another, over the shifting and anxious face of western Europe—a continent betwixt and between these days, a continent out of gear perhaps, rickety Britain with its
fairy fantasies, young France, half macho, half poet-and-peasant, Switzerland of the fanatic roller-skaters, Italy of the sham horse and the real live
monks, Yugoslavia with its lid tippling and clanking, like a kettle on the
boil.

"Come far?" inquired the Montenegrin, lighting a short cigar. Not so
far, I thought: but over the ridge before us, wrapped in their Godless
silence, stood the mountains of Albania.

Oil on Granite

ABERDEEN, SCOTLAND

For my tastes (but then I love the *brio* of capitalism in the raw) the harbor of Aberdeen is marvellous to see in the evening. It is not a big harbor, two artificial inlets attached to the mouth of the Dee and protected by a breakwater against the open sea, but it is always in motion. The rusty flotillas of fishing-boats may be asleep, their blur of masts and funnels illuminated only by a few masthead lights, but the oil docks all around are brilliantly awake. The tall storage tanks glitter in the floodlights. The ungainly supply-boats, humped up forward, elongated aft, hum at their quays. From the shrouded shape of a vessel in the yards, towered over by derricks, a fireworks spray of oxy-acetylene showers through the dusk.

There are hissing, clanging and thumping noises, the pilot launch scuds here and there, the hulk of a freighter heaves itself cautiously from a quay, the Orkney steamer slips away down the navigation channel, exchanging incomprehensible Scotticisms with the harbormen in their tower. Out at sea four or five supply-boats lie beneath their riding lights, and sometimes a helicopter comes clanking in from the east, heavily over the docks towards the airport.

Aberdeen is the chief support base for the North Sea oil operations. Here are the supply-ships, the depots, the aircraft, the electronics, the technical agencies, which sustain the storm-battered rigs and platforms far out at sea. This is capitalist enterprise at its most dazzling and pugnacious, and the harbor quay at Aberdeen is one of the last places in the

British Isles where you may feel the authentic tingle of get-rich-quick. Thousands of millions of pounds are invested in these craft and machineries; skills from a dozen nations are concentrated here; through this conduit Americans, Englishmen, Frenchmen, Dutchmen, Spaniards, Italians, Greeks, Norwegians, Swedes, Germans, pass in a ceaseless traffic to and from the oilfields out of sight.

Yet behind the harbor, as night falls, the city of Aberdeen stands grave and grey. A tower or two, of kirk or civic pile, stand sentinel beyond the cranes, like keepers of the public conscience, but there are no skyscrapers, revolving restaurants on towers, neon lights or blazing late-night stores. No thump of go-go echoes down Mill Brae or Rennies Wynd. Aberdeen seems hardly more than a backdrop to the performance on its own quays, for though this venerable burgh has long joined the roster of the boom towns, Kimberley to Abu Dhabi, it remains tentative to the experience. Other towns have gold rushes or silver strikes: Aberdeen's is a distinctly granite bonanza.

−o / o / o−

Handsome, civilized, diligent, granite, Aberdeen has never been rich before, but has always been canny. Until the oil strikes it lived by fishing and agriculture, and though it knew much poverty and unemployment in the bad old days, it never let its standards slip. Its very substance seemed indestructible, so that its buildings never looked either old or new, never particularly shabby, never noticeably opulent.

It is very hard to date a building in Aberdeen, so easily does one century blend into the next, and very hard to place a citizen, so decorously but economically does nearly everyone dress. The grandest houses in town, the severe granite villas built for the trawler-owners at the turn of the century, are scarcely ostentatious: the old fishing quarter of Footdee, jumbled on the shore beside the harbor, is still occupied by fishing families and dockyard workers, but has been done up bijou-style by the municipality, with concrete bowls for shrubberies, and dainty cobbled yards.

The town stands on the edge of the moors, a city of 200,000 halfway from Edinburgh to John O'Groats. Here the produce of the eastern Highlands traditionally comes to market, here the fish of the north are frozen, whisked away to London or turned into malodorous byproducts. Aberdeen is deeply rooted. Its Shore Porters' Society was established in 1498 ("for the commone profit of the tone according to the Ald louable

consuetude and law of this Burghe"). Its Common Good fund was be-
queathed to it by Robert the Bruce. Its Walker Park was originally created
for the grazing of lighthouse keepers' cattle. Its Gothic Auld Brig o'
Balgownie was so well-endowed by a seventeenth-century benefactor that
when they needed to build a new bridge, two centuries later, the cost was
easily covered. Aberdeen's history is rich in arcane Scottish legends and
allusions: Dr. Johnson indeed found it all a bit *too* Scottish.

Little has really changed since his day, I would imagine, at the auction
by which, each morning at 8 a.m., the trawlers dispose of their catch. The
boats, rimmed still with frost and ice from the fishing grounds, mostly
look antique themselves, and the fishermen look altogether timeless, stalwart, comely men, their faces rigid in the truest Scottish mold, unhurried,
polite; and there the fish of the cold seas lie as they always did, cod, hake
and flatfish, glistening in their wooden crates; and through all the hub-
bub, the slithering of seaboots, the clattering of boxes, the gutturals of
badinage, the chugging of engines, the shrieking of seabirds, the slurping
of tea from enamel mugs, white-coated auctioneers immemorially grunt
their prices, and lorries rumble away over the cobbled quays.

It is an interesting but not an exhilarating scene, but then Aberdeen is
not built for exuberance. It is not, as one of its servants remarked to me, a
fizzy town. It has been ruled for thirty years by estimable Labour councils,
and even the excitements of Scottish nationalism have scarcely disturbed
its orthodoxy—the only nationalist emblems I saw in town were the Welsh
ones I flaunt on my own car. "What's the suicide rate?" I asked one of
the city spokesmen, conjecturing a certain *ennui* to these arrangements,
but this was a question he particularly welcomed, for it is the lowest in
Great Britain.

The crime rate is the lowest, too, and the juvenile delinquency rate,
and the vandalism rate, and the unemployment rate: and the educational
standards are the highest, and the long beach promenade is entirely un-
vulgarized, and the town has won the Britain in Bloom contest so often
that it has tactfully withdrawn from the contest. Aberdeen has an enterprising arts center, municipally supported, and its high-rise buildings
have been tastefully held in check, and its industrial development is dis-
creetly zoned, and altogether it is in many ways the best of all possible
burghs—*"Beriall of all tounis,"* as one of its eulogists suggested long ago,
"the lamp of bewtie, bountie and blythness. . . ."

It is also very self-assured, not to say complacent, and is not much put out by the sniggers of visiting reporters. Embedded in the fabric of Marischal College (the second largest granite building in the world—largest of all if you forget the Escorial, as some guide books conveniently do) there is an ancient inscribed stone, all that is left of the medieval college building. The official motto of Aberdeen is "Bon Accord," but I think this gnomic announcement very much more apposite. "THEY HAIF SAID," it growls, and answers itself, "WHAT SAY THEY. LAT YAME SAY."

– o / o / o –

Upon this hoary and provident town the juggernaut of oil has fallen more or less out of the sky. Until I went to Aberdeen I had no conception of its scale. Seen against so stolid a setting, it is staggering. One oil person actually apologized to me for a development that cost a mere million: anything less than a billion or two is hardly worth mentioning. There is nothing modest to the North Sea oil affair. All is vast, dear and dangerous.

It is like a war, and billeted upon Aberdeen, as alien to the city as the officers of some occupying army, are the staffs and technical corps of the campaign. This is the intelligence base of the North Sea operations, the logistical center, the technical depot: here too are all the auxiliaries, financiers to camp followers, landladies to economists. The local oil directory lists them all, and their very entries on the page are like a roll-call of regiments, drawn from all corners of some great alliance, and assembled beneath their several flags in this unlikely salient.

Some are old concerns, like the Shore Porters' Society, which has deftly adapted to new consuetudes. Some are altogether contemporary, like The Analysts (North Sea) Inc., whose function is described as "computerized well-logging." These are firms who specialize in video systems, light marker buoys, diamond bits, sub-surface surveys, helium supplies, air refuelling systems, data acquisition, cathodic protection. There are divers, tug-owners, helicopter pilots, ship-repairers. There are Royleen Partners, who offer Furnished Flats for Single Oil Men. Altogether some 250 service companies have followed the oil giants to Aberdeen, and are now distributed, flashing, ticking and computerizing, among the quays, offices and industrial estates of the old town.

Aberdeen's airport is shortly to be rebuilt, but at the moment it is a messy tumble of huts and congested car-parks deposited beside a housing estate at Dyce. Unprepossessing as it is, though, it is astonishingly vigorous. They say it is now the busiest helicopter base in the world, its big Sikorskys lumbering off at all hours northwards and eastwards to the rigs, and six scheduled jets arrive each day from London. Its waiting rooms are never empty, for here the infantry of the oil industry, the men who do the dirty jobs on the rigs, are assembled and posted. They are of all nationalities, all sizes, all styles, a few preposterously in Texan hats and studded boots, many more looking less swaggering than homesick. Often they never see Aberdeen at all, but are helicoptered direct from Dyce to the rigs at sea, or bundled off that afternoon to the Shetlands.

To many of them Aberdeen is only a name anyway, just another stop in their circuit of the world's oilfields, Arabian Gulf to Indonesia, Alaska to Brazil. They are there merely to make lots of money, by the truest principles of *laissez faire*. Not all the rigs are unionized, and a man can work out there as long as he likes, as dangerously as he is willing, before returning to Louisiana, Sicily or Galicia with blistered hands and a fine fat check. They are like pilgrims from another age, the transit passengers at Dyce: Aberdeen watches them pass not enviously, I think, but perhaps a little wistfully.

– o / o / o –

For Aberdeen's response to bonanza has been essentially wary. It has kept the whole phenomenon, for better or for worse, at arm's length. Many of the local firms were slow to adapt, so that expertise of all kinds was brought in from abroad: many more were bewildered by the high wages forced on them by the oil firms. On the other hand the City Fathers presciently determined that their fine old town would not be degraded by it all. Planning restrictions were inflexible. New factories were sternly zoned. The mile-long esplanade of Union Street, the main thoroughfare of the city, remains as sober, as thrifty, as firmly supervised by the Salvation Army Citadel at one end, the old Free Church College at the other, as ever it was before the companies came. And all the time, in its measured way, Aberdeen was taking what it could.

Union Street may not have changed much, but a subtle and restrained suggestion of *richesse,* all the same, now runs through the civic life, noticeable in luxurious offices, beautifully maintained schools, new equipment, a general sense of that ease and even temper which comes, as we all know, from having a bit of money in the bank. In Aberdeen there is none of the seedy stagnancy inescapable in English cities: the car-wash machine will be the very latest kind, the canteen floor will be carpeted, the hand-outs are lavish and BMWs are two a penny.

Such a place provides, I would think, an almost perfect infrastructure for an explosively aggressive international industry. Its citizens are unfailingly courteous, and highly competent. All its systems seem to work. Nothing could be more soothingly efficient than the organization of Mr. Foreman, the head waiter at the Station Hotel, whose splendid old-fashioned breakfasts welcomed me each day after my morning walk along the promenade: nothing could be more reassuring than the punctual orderly progress of the double-deckers one after the other along Union Street, as though time itself has been taken in hand by the Lord Provost and his councillors up at the Town House.

−o / o / o−

Furious by contrast is the momentum of North Sea oil, full of risk and skull-dug, and strange are the forms and idioms which storm through Aberdeen these days. Oil people are flamboyantly conscious of their own images, and North Sea technology is so new that it burgeons always with the vivid and the unexpected.

Take the names of the rigs, fields and supply-boats which, emblazoned on shiny publicity charts, or stamped on packing cases, are inescapable in Aberdeen. If Aberdonians had named them they would perhaps commemorate local theologians or social economists, but they were christened by people of gaudier temperament, and have gustier names: Cormorant, Josephine, Piper, Auk, Oil Hunter, Active King, Dogger Shore, Wimpey Sea-Fox.

Take the colors and symbols of it all, the bright yellows, blues and reds of the storage tanks around the docks, the glaring paintwork of the supply-boats, the company flags and totems, the hefty whirring helicopters, the images of the great rigs beyond the horizon.

Or take the shapes! In the dock depots at Aberdeen they store all the spare equipment for the rigs, colossal inventories of implements and gadgetry, stacked and tabulated for instant dispatch by the supply-ships waiting always at the quay. They reminded me of tropical markets, so exotic were their forms and silhouettes: marker buoys like long rigid eels, bits of drills like vegetables or sea-urchins, steel ribs and teeth and finger-joints, huge rig anchors in whale shapes or shark forms, diamond bits casketed like precious fetishes, primitive art in links or bolts or casings.

There is beauty here. It is the beauty of power and innovation, which inspired Turner in his day, but is hard to find in modern Britain. It is the brutal beauty of competitive enterprise: men racing each other, the snatch for profit, the outpouring of colossal resources in the hope of still more immense returns. It suits this hard northern coastline, where the wild storms sweep in from the sea, and where once the Aberdeen clippers sailed out to capture the prizes of the tea trade. Oil magnates may have their doubts about London, even about Edinburgh, but they can hardly quarrel with Aberdeen.

The granite buildings of the city, so somber in the rain, glitter slightly in the sunshine, because they are impregnated with mica—Fool's Gold, as the American panhandlers used to call it. When I suggested to one Aberdonian that this might offer a cautionary analogy for the city, he dismissed the notion very Aberdonianly.

$$-o\,/\,o\,/\,o-$$

"They do things," he said, "different over there." If there is one aspect of Aberdeen that probably differentiates it from every other boom town in the history of booms, it is a quality of skeptical reserve. Scarcely a soul I met in the town failed to mention that the oil wouldna last for ever. "It canna last for ever. The future willna take care of itself."

This is a fragile boom. The oil certainly will *not* last for ever. The companies may at a pinch withdraw. If the world price of oil fell the fields would not be worth working anyway. The whole adventure might fizzle out. Those grand offices might be up for rent, those queer ships might sail away to Hamburg or Stavanger, the last helicopter might clatter off once and for all, Mr. Jamieson at the Post Office might find no more customers for his Datapost Same-Day Delivery Service to New York. Aberdeen might become once more only a fishing, market and university town, away up there between the Highlands and the sea.

They have thought of that. Aberdeen has always specialized in derived science—drawing intellectual conclusions from practical premises. It specialized long ago in what to do with fish, how to farm the sea, how best to grow things, how best to feed things—all subjects which, filtered through the academic process, sprang directly from the nature and needs of the place. Now its formidable university departments and research institutes have applied their powers to the after-uses of oil. Whatever happens to the oilfields themselves, Aberdeen plans to remain a world center of oil technology. Its labs and engineering shops have been involved with North Sea oil from the start, and all the newly developed ideas about offshore oil have been catalyzed and conceptualized here. Whatever happens, Aberdonians aim to keep a perpetual bonus from the North Sea, as rich and lasting as Robert the Bruce's bequest, as useful as the Brig o' Balgownie endowment fund.

There is no denying that all this prudent foresight makes Aberdeen one of the less exciting of boom towns. It is like betting on a favorite, or rather not betting at all. You might spend a day shopping in Aberdeen, and never know about that dazzle of enterprise down at the docks. You might take afternoon tea at Fraser's (Orkney butter, Kraft's strawberry jam) and never realize that oil has been found at all. There is none of that intoxication of high stakes and opportunism, that tang of the bazaar, that joyous splurge of *nouveau riche,* which enlivens such places in less calculating climes. There is no *suddenness* to Aberdeen. The ecstasy rate, I would say, is very low.

But when I suggested to the same prickly citizen that some people might think these reactions a little, well, dull, he did not seem to care much what they thought. He scoffed. "WHAT SAY THEY," he retorted, or thereabouts, "LET YAME SAY."

What They Had To Offer

MIAMI, U.S.A.

"Well, what have you guys got to offer us?" inquired the early American settlers beside the Miami River, of the Seminole Indians who manifested themselves out of the swamp. The Indians slapped their thighs. What *hadn't* they got to offer? Alligator tails, egret feathers, deer hides, shrimps—you name it! The pioneers were reassured, hacked out estates for themselves upon the foreshore, and are commemorated now in avenues, condominiums and haughty dynastic connections.

Such, 130 years ago, were the unlikely opportunities for success on this unpromising shore, and even now there is something inherently unconvincing about the existence of Greater Miami, strung out in such straggling profusion, NE 215 Street to SW 392, between the soggy Everglades and the Ocean. Who could possibly want to live, one wonders, in such a hole? What could it possibly be for? The climate is warm, of course, the beaches are grand, the geographical location is convenient; but they seem insufficient *raisons d'être,* all the same, for one of the most explosively vital, profitable, magnetic and repellent places on the face of the earth.

And as with causes, so with presence. Miami has no particular presence. It is like a vast jelly, flattened by some kitchen catastrophe and squashed out of all recognizable mold. It is utterly inorganic. Its highest ground is a bump in a park created by the burying of surplus construction machinery, half its islands are artificial, and even its native tropicalness has been more or less expunged: if ever you see a peeling Conradian building beneath a banyan tree, it is sure to be listed for demolition, and the only reminder of the Everglades is the flock of turkey vultures habitually wheeling bewildered around the roof of the Dade County Courthouse.

By normal standards it is hardly a city at all, but rather an amoebic co-agulation of separate settlements, and Greater Miami is the only metropolis of my acquaintance whose inhabitants are likely to speak of it by the name of its parent county, Dade County, which as everyone knows is one of the most violently lawless in the United States, and is appositely named for the late Major Francis Dade, mugged here by Indians in 1835. Miami has no corporate personality, and all recent attempts by its publicists to give it an image have failed, neither the slogan "Miami is for Me," nor the title "Magic City," nor the unnerving municipally recommended drink called the Miami Whammy having seized the world's imagination.

Yet almost everyone on earth, offered the name of this city, has a vision of the place; and even the baffled traveller on the spot, groping through its obfuscatory street arrangements (avenues, courts and places run east and west, roads and drives go where they like)—even the most impressionistic of wanderers cannot escape its fascination. It is the most peculiar of the great cities of America, and the hardest to pin down.

$-o\,/\,o\,/\,o-$

Visually, or aesthetically, Miami seems uncertain as to what decade we have reached. From my high hotel window the clumped downtown towers of the city certainly look contemporary enough, with modish silhouettes in every stage of construction, and for the most part the wide waterfront too seems powerfully of the 1980s—the causeways to Miami Beach all astream with traffic or smoothly opening their bascules to let the boats pass through, the coves encrusted with yacht marinas, the tall condominiums stretching away down coast and island as far as the eye can see. But in the foreground of the scene, lined up bow to stern along the dockside lies a string of great cruise liners, white and blue and all beflagged, which appear to have strayed here from another period altogether, the age of the ocean greyhounds—and Great Scott, look, here there comes roaring fussily over Biscayne Boulevard a genuine old-fashioned white flying boat, which splutters a bit, waggles its wings, and lands on its station beside Watson Island looking for all the world like a Pan Am poster of the 1930s!

On the whole, in this conflict of the decades, the thirties win. Hardly anything in this city is older than our century, but somehow nothing feels particularly new either, not even the present splurge of hotels and banks and condominiums, not even the high-rise building with the square hole in the side of it. This is perhaps because Miami's one period of style came between the two World Wars, and so amorphous has been its development ever since, so varied are its driving impulses, that the flamboyances of today make little impact on the general manner of things. What with the palm trees and the cruise ships, the mock-Italian villas and Dorothy Lamour on at the Eden Roc, the predominant effect of this town remains, for me at least, one of unidentifiable 1930ish jumble.

Much of it has lately *been* identified, actually, and given learned names like Mediterranean Eclectic, Depression Moderne and Tropical Deco. Thus it turns out to everyone's surprise, for instance, that the hitherto unnoticed hotels and apartment blocks standing cheek by jowl along Miami Beach, all wrought-iron flamingos and loony roof ornaments, are historical monuments to be discussed on lecture tours. Upon their porches dear old Jewish couples, winter habitués of the Cardozo or the Carlyle for more years than they care to remember, sit amazed to discover that they have been staying in an Art Form all this time!

Most thirtyish of all, though, is the Miami River itself, the beginning of all things in this city; for this narrow jumbled waterway, generally invisible as it makes its way stealthily beneath the city's bridges, seems to ignore the 1980s altogether. Stacked along its whole length with boatyards, houseboats, docks, and shambled mooring places, with white freighters from the Cayman Islands and smugglers' boats seized by customs, everything about it speaks of less homogenized, more stylish times. Here Lana Turner and Errol Flynn used to keep their yachts, here Spencer Tracy made a movie, and nothing much has changed since their days. It reminds me sometimes of the Singapore River, and sometimes of Chicago, and is much the best thing to see in Miami, if you can only find it.

— o / o / o —

But then nobody pretends that Miami is a city to look at; it is a city to be in. Waves and waves, tides and tides of immigrants have beaten upon this shore since Henry Flagler, in 1896, drove his Florida East Coast Railway down to these parts and opened the place up for tourism and settlement. Today Miami is an ethnic blur. The Dade authorities tell me that in 1980 there were about 681,000 non-Hispanic whites in the county, and 581,000 Hispanics, and 280,000 blacks, and 12,000 Asians, and 1,700 Indians; but there were 69,000 that they could define only as Others. People black, brown, yellow, many shades of white, green for all I know, walk these boulevards. Tongues beyond number are heard—a dozen kinds of Spanish for a start, a dozen kinds of American English, too, slithery Creole of Haiti, rustic dialects of Barbados or the Caymans, vibrant Rio Portuguese or British Honduran English, which seems to be a sort of Swedish-accented Australian. I was driving through the black quarter of Overtown one night when I heard an ominous cry directed at me, repeated time and time again through the darkness: Rungway, Rungway, those black men yelled at me, and I wondered uneasily what arcane curse it could be, until I realized I was driving incorrectly down a one-way street.

Miami has long since displaced New York as the promised land of the immigrants: Bring me your dispossessed plutocrats, deported jailbirds, money launderers, disinherited dictators, drug smugglers, secret agents, supporters of the Shah, titled European interior decorators, pastors of obscure Caribbean sects, world-weary sheikhs, crooks, fools, charlatans and dupes all yearning to breathe free! Among a recent group of illegal immigrants arriving in Miami in half-waterlogged boats from the Bahamas were a number of Bangladeshi, who found this the most convenient way of concluding their 9000-mile journey to the United States, and during my own week in the place I encountered in casual contact people from Sri Lanka, Peru, Australia, Spain, Brazil, the Philippines, Sweden, France, Bolivia, Nicaragua and Iran.

Here and there within the maelstrom, nevertheless, the original Miamians still hold their heads above water: the Anglos, as Miami people call all English-speaking Americans—the Real Americans, as they sometimes add. Many of them live, as Real Americans tend to, far, far away among remote suburban shopping malls, and are never seen by visitors. Others emerge now and then to fulfill their traditional ethnic roles—producing the *Miami Herald,* for instance, presiding over law courts, attending opera balls, ministering at the Trinity Episcopal Cathedral (the senior warden of which is Rear Admiral Louis J. Kirn, and the hall of which is hung with the massed tartans of the Scottish clans); or for that matter, when I was in Miami, standing in patient lines around the Orange Bowl Stadium, like victims of some unreported persecution, to get their free cheese from the federal surplus.

For they do have the air of a threatened minority. They are old on the average, they have problems enough about Social Security, and many of them feel themselves unable to cope with the merciless pressure of multi-racialism, polylingualese, values they feel to be alien, forms they cannot grasp. They make the old joke about the last American to leave the city—"please lower the flag"—and pointedly decline to say good morning in Spanish. They remind me of English people in South Africa, caught between the awful passions of blacks and Afrikaners, feeling themselves at once superior, superfluous and ill done by. Of course the rich Anglos of Miami are still very rich, and very powerful, but you would not know it, for somehow even they seem essentially on the fringe of things these days, playing with their catamarans on the bay, or huddled over small talk in expensive restaurants, pretending to prefer *la nouvelle cuisine.*

– o / o / o –

And outshining them all these days, no doubt about it, stand the Cubans. They are the stars of Miami now. They occupy the center of the stage, and must occupy the center of this essay too. Their language is the most aggressive, their culture the most striking, and into all the corridors of Miami consequence, City Hall to Florida Philharmonic, Cubans have made their way. They set the tone of downtown Miami—probably the liveliest downtown in America, but lively in a purely Hispanic way, the fretted way, the loud but oddly sad-eyed way, that goes with black beans and inverted exclamation marks. Small frilly shops flourish, Spanish music booms across the *café con leche,* shirt-sleeved salesmen shrug their shoulders morosely when you say you've seen the same binoculars at half the price around the corner, and into grand financial buildings distinguished mournful-looking men step guardedly, murmuring instructions over their shoulders to obsequious aides.

To some degree, of course, this is an American epitome. The Latinization of the United States proceeds helter-skelter, as year by year invasions of Puerto Ricans, Mexicans, Cubans change the nature of the Republic as absolutely as did the millions of European immigrants in the nineteenth century. But in Miami the process has a sad extra dimension, specifically because of the Cubans. For the most part they did not want to come, and their Miami is hardly more than a surrogate Havana. To the old excitement of the melting pot Miami adds harsher elements of resentment, regret and recrimination.

Cuba and Miami have loved and hated each other for ages. It was from Miami that the envoys of the Mob sailed out to commandeer the gaming joints, brothels and ancillary rackets of Batista's Havana; and to Miami in return have come successive wages—generations by now—of anti-Castro dissidents, from the rich and educated political exiles who fled the Communist revolution in the first place, to the poor deadbeats and rejected thugs let loose by Fidel Castro in the boatlift from Mariel in 1980. Stunningly successful though the Cubans have been in Miami, they strike me as a tragic community even now; for in this generation at least they remain besotted by their betrayed and beloved Cuba.

Much the best-known man in Cuban Miami is José Martí, who though he died in the cause of Cuban independence eighty-eight years ago, lives on here inescapably, an inherited inspiration, sometimes I dare say getting vaguer in the public mind, but periodically jerked into clarity again by a new memorial or an anniversary. He is ubiquitous especially along Calle Ocho, SW 8 Street, "Little Havana," and there around his ghostly presence all the symptoms of exileness coalesce. Monuments to dead heroes or epic enterprises abound, old men in hats play immemorial gambling games of the homeland, there is an Office in Exile of the City of Santiago de Cuba, and in countless tumultuous restaurants elderly waiters, pausing in their delivery of the black beans, recall apprenticeships in old Havana.

I called one afternoon upon the activists of Alpha 66, the most visible of the exiled Cuban resistance groups, who plot perpetually the overthrow of Fidel Castro (and are not to be confused with Omega 7 or the Cuban National Movement, still less the Cuban Dental Association in Exile, Inc.). Their office, as it happened, had just been scorched by the incendiary device of some rival outfit, but they seemed undeterred. Photographs of grim freedom fighters lined its walls; our talk was all of infiltration, sabotage and subversion; and on the vast wall-map the locations of Castro's prisons were fiercely pinpointed. A former prison inmate was at hand too, looking ill and angry, to tell me of his experiences, and now and then vividly guerrilla-like men stalked through the room, on the way perhaps to secret embarkation points, or more probably to week-end training camps in the Everglades. "We are always on the move," said the spokesman in commentary as they passed, *"always ready to go back!"*

Poor guerrillas! I was sorry for them, so burning was their obsession, so apparently forlorn their dream. I was even a little sorry for the top Miami

Cuban of them all, the elegant Raul P. Masvidal, when he welcomed me to his exquisitely carriage-trade Biscayne Bank ("Account relationships considered," as its advertisements say, "of over $50,000"). An exile since the early 1960s, a Bay of Pigs recruit, Masvidal has lived in New York and Madrid, and during the past decade in Miami he has achieved social and economic celebrity. Few public events are complete without him, few enterprises can afford to ignore him, rumor has his finger in political pies from Dade to D.C. Yet as he sat there that morning in his office, looking less like a financier than a rather overworked operatic tenor, he sounded to me, I thought, more wistful than exultant. He missed his homeland still, he told me. He was concerned about the Americanization of his children. Besides, he really wanted to be president, not just of the Biscayne Bank, but of the Cuban Republic.

–o/o/o–

I was accompanied to Alpha 66 that day by a bodyguard from Dominica, holding an umbrella—my taxi driver, actually. He was not at his ease, for he does not like Cubans, and while I interviewed the maquis he sat in an armchair looking glum and apprehensive. "Them Cubans can certainly talk," he said as we left. "Yappety-yappety-yap—that's what Cubans is all about."

But then Cubans, I dare say, do not like Dominicans, either. Nobody in Miami cares very much for anybody else, so far as I can see, and like so many Darwinian species the communities of Miami are for ever driving each other from their habitats, in an evolutionary way: as one race enters a district, another leaves; white gives way to brown, brown to black; Episcopalian churches having been outperformed by shrines to Our Lady of Montserrat, in comes the One-Way Church of God's Witness to clear the boards again.

There never was so caste-ridden a city, for all its separate divisions are themselves infinitely subdivided. Even the Cubans, who seem to their enemies and rivals so monolithically united, are in fact mortally split, because the generation that is now growing into maturity, like Mr. Masvidal's children, no longer heeds the old shibboleths of the island tradition. The sons of the exiles feel themselves exiles no more, tend to speak Spanglish at best, frequently cultivate the company of blonde Protestants, prefer hamburgers to black beans, English TV to Spanish, and so threaten to undermine the whole hierarchy built up so painstakingly by their elders.

Within the beleaguered Anglo community, too, as always, minuscule gradations of social nuance divide the ruling class. Miami Shores or Miami Springs? Coral Gables or Coconut Grove? Which *end* of Coral Gables? How *long* at Coconut Grove? Who was his father, and why didn't they make the Greater Miami Social Register? One suburb is Old Money, another is New Money (and a third is whispered to be Drug Money, but that's only since the Hispanics moved in of course . . .).

And among the various communities of the colored poor, distributed over miles and miles of indistinguishable grid, in bungalows and tenements and the clapboard huts they call shotgun houses—you could shoot a bullet easy front to back—in all that formless mass of poor Miami, tight loyal communities cluster around their origins, their friends and their cultures. On my first Sunday in Miami I was taken on a tour of Overtown and Liberty City, the two principal black quarters, and never did I feel such a succession of separate affinities, one after another across town.

We visited, for a start, a video arcade in Overtown where, not so long before, an innocent black man had been shot dead by a Cuban policeman, starting an ugly riot. It seemed to me a genial kind of place. I had a hamburger, small boys steadfastly played the machines, the manager chatted agreeably. Presently behind the easy welcome, though, I sensed the presence of a watchful brotherhood all around—eyes looking at me through the back door, silent appraisals from the loungers in the street—a suggestion of mesh-like collusion which made me feel that all down 14 Street people already knew of my presence there, and had been told by ethnic code or semaphore to treat me nice.

We went to Little Haiti, too, and places where Hondurans gathered, and we called upon Dominicans, and bumped into Bahamians, and ended up in a boarding house, in the shadow of Interstate 95, which was especially frequented by Jamaicans. Here the fellowship was of a heartier kind. Ah, what jolly ladies sat there in their flowered dresses and bedroom slippers amidst the potted palms! What hilarious jokes they shared, what dear friends they remembered, and how their laughter defied the rumble of the expressway outside the window, when all unexpected Thomas and Alicia, straight from Kingston, man, true thing, came banging on the door, loaded up with tote bags of duty-free rum, to make that modest sitting room, hung all about with holy texts and posters of Montego Bay, a very oasis of companionship in the heart of the loveless city!

−o / o / o −

On·the day I arrived in Miami they buried Meyer Lansky, for many years the financial genius of the Mob. Nobody mourned him more sincerely than I, for I had hoped to interview him about the city: as a retired businessman from the North he was an archetypal Miami resident of the traditional kind, and there is nothing like Old Money for civic insight. As it was, at least I visited his burial place in Mount Nebo Cemetery ("Guarded By Attack Dogs"): but there was nothing to mark the spot, only a diligently stamped-down plot of earth, as though the mourners had trodden it over and over again with the heels of their shoes, just in case.

Mobsters and Miami used to go together: Al Capone died here, and long before they smuggled drugs or immigrants into this city, they smuggled bootleg whiskey. Today the focus of immorality is harder to define, but the villainy remains all right—villainy almost unimaginable, subtler and slimier than ever the old mobs knew. The drug-smuggling outfits of Miami are like multinational corporations, *Fortune*-listable, and if we are to believe the investigative reporters Miami is riddled with corruption from top to bottom. Nobody offered to bribe me, alas, but I did feel a frisson of menace in Miami now and then: in the downtown flophouse area, for example, where the emaciated solitaries, drug-hazed and wine-sozzled, all looked as though they would rape me if they had the energy; or on Overtown street corners sometimes, where the hawkers of coke and pot all looked as though they would murder me, if they could think of a reason; or when a magnate's bodyguard, with a droopy moustache and a tight-buttoned suit, beckoned me peremptorily across a room, *Tch, Tch,* with a click of his fingers; or most disturbingly of all, perhaps, just reading the newspapers in the snug security of my hotel bedroom, and imagining all the vice, savagery and mayhem happening right then in the city down below—all the murderers and extortioners, the rapers and the flashers, the terrorist bombers, the crooked judges, the criminal policemen, the drug-based billionaires, who appeared in the columns of the *Herald* during my brief stay in town.

All the same, while it is true that I met plenty of men in Miami from whom I would hesitate to buy a second-hand machine-gun, all in all I was struck less by the wickedness of the place than by its resilient decency. Nobody did rape me, or throw my carcass in the Miami River. On the contrary, everybody I met was disappointingly polite. Courtly Cubans told me the story of José Martí, charming Jews reminisced about Mr. Lansky, hospitable Anglos urged me to try the *coquille Saint-Jacques,* and everywhere in colored Miami, beneath the photographs of Martin Luther King or the oleographs of the Virgin Mary, I came across homely kindness and reassuring family disciplines—"You girl, why you got no shoes on? What's this lady goin' to think, you wearing no shoes? You get those shoes on, 'fore I get angry, you hear me?"

For even in Dade County the innocent are always with us; and as a matter of fact the Miami Haitians are sometimes so innocent that their own court lawyers refuse to believe their testimony, finding it incredible that any defendant should stick so absolutely to the truth.

–o / o / o–

It seems unlikely, I know, but all this mishmash, all these contradictions and exceptions, add up to an impression of immense if transient power. Miami's very diffusion paradoxically makes for fizz and vivacity, if hardly for anything more majestic. This is the open city *in excelsis,* all horizontal, all laid back, and the irrepressible forces of finance, influence, ambition and skullduggery are perpetually rushing through it. Into the man-made port of Dodge Island, one of the busiest in America, the hideous container ships stream night and day, scurried about by futuristic tugs and fallen upon by terrific gantry cranes. At the international airport, one of the busiest in the world, seventy-eight scheduled airlines fly in and out. On Brickell Avenue banks of a dozen nations maintain their gleaming offices, and on NW 79 Street you will find the Fiji Tourism Board.

All this, from those egret plumes and alligator tails! But productively speaking Miami has not much more to offer now than it had in the 1850s. It does not exactly produce things: it arranges things, and hides things, and soothes things, and makes things easier, and faster, and more entertaining, and more profitable. It will tranship your cars to Venezuela, or process your data, or hatch your revolution, or launder your bills, or give you a good time on Miami Beach, or arrange a million-dollar bond so that you can skip away home to Colombia. It has conjured its own materials, out of nothing, and so has turned itself into one of the world cities, one of the handful of places that exert their authority, in one form or another, far beyond their own national boundaries.

So *that's* what it's for! It is the Beirut of the 1980s. They used to liken Beirut to the bumble-bee, which aerodynamically ought to be flightless, and perhaps Miami, being equally evanescent and improbable, may one day come to earth too. In the meantime its destiny seems to be in the hands of those Cubans, and God knows what they will do with it. They may declare its independence, or use it as a base for the domination of the USA, or perhaps, as they are metamorphosed into Real Americans themselves, make it the new All-American City. Or they may take it back to Cuba with them.

Trans-Texan

AN AMERICAN JOURNEY

It was like entering another, and more nationalistic, country—like entering France, say, out of Switzerland. The moment I crossed the Red River out of Oklahoma, the nationality of Texas assaulted me almost xenophobically, and I seemed to be passing into another sensibility, another historical experience, another scale of values perhaps. I was about to drive all the way down US 281, one of the several highways which run clean across Texas north to south: not because it is the fastest of them or the most important, or even I dare say the most scenic, but because it is one of the oldest of all the tracks by which the original Texans, long ago, drove their cattle northward to Kansas City and the rich markets of the north. Nobody seems quite sure which was actually the Chisholm Trail, the most famous of these routes: but we can be quite certain that along the line of US 281 generations of herdsmen came and went, and that up and down it, too, so to speak, passed many of those impulses, influences and instincts which brought Texas to its own manifest destiny, and united it with the greater Republic to the north.

It is rather more than 600 miles down 281, from Red River in the north to Rio Grande in the south, across pleasant flatland counties with names like Jack or Archer, through the wooded hill country of the center, across the wider rolling ranchlands south of San Antonio into the tropic territories of the Rio Grande valley, where the palm trees stand in lordly enfilade, where the fruit and vegetables grow like lush weeds, and there seems to hang upon the very air some potent radiation of the south.

Yet hardly was I over that bridge when all the conventional shapes and symptoms of Texas rose up around me: massed bluebonnets on the verges, smells of sage and barbecue, Stetson-hatted heads silhouetted through the rear windows of pick-ups, horses corraled in village yards, cattle roaming like wild beasts over evidently limitless ranges, the indefatigable shapes of Texan oil-pumps, the uncontrollable shapes of Texan countrymen, the shape of Texas itself, that asymmetrical lump of tenderloin on maps and guides, on road signs and posters, on T-shirts and dishcloths and key-rings in souvenir shops and windows. The weather of Texas variously lifted my heart and squashed my spirits. From earth and air, creek and camper, I was hounded by the curse of Texas, country and western music.

So I began my journey, assaulted by Texanity, and the great sky of Texas seemed to close like a door behind me, as though I were in some separate cosmos now, spinning to another rhythm, tugged by different laws of gravity.

−o / o / o−

"Good grief!" cried the girl at the bank at Wichita Falls, "Wales! Do you hear that, Mary-Lou?" But without a second thought she pressed a computer button for instant confirmation that my bank account in Llanystumdwy was in credit, and handed me my money.

The insularity of Texas has always entertained travellers, coupled as it is with extreme technical sophistication, and Texans of course love to make the most of it, flying their flag as if it were still their own republican emblem, using their dialect like another language. The scale of everything certainly contributes to the illusion: often Texas felt to me not even like a country, but like a continent of its own, and 281 suggested to me the sort of strategic thoroughfare that European wars were fought for, and frontiers adjusted to accommodate.

Yet Texas is not in the least separate really: even the Texanest of Texan families must have come here from somewhere else not so very long ago, and hardly a nation of Europe has not contributed to the style that advertises itself to the world nowadays as Texan to the core. As the writer Philip Bailey once said of America as a whole, in Texas there is "something good and bad of every land," and all along Route 281, down the decades, immigrants from many parts have set up shop, dug down roots, turned themselves into something of Texas and Texas into a little of themselves.

You could hardly call something so huge as Texas microcosmic, and the landscape itself did not often remind me of other countries, being purely American I thought in its ever-present hint of disappointment or disillusionment, or what you might call its majestic monotony (to be honest with you, there is more beautiful scenery within five miles of Llanystumdwy than there is down the length of US 281). But time and again social analogies, especially in the northern counties, put me in mind of older nations far away. Those shacks littered with old cars and rusty ploughs, those abandoned stores along the highway, those half-deserted hamlets of the back-country—all irresistibly suggested to me, set as they were against so vast and flat a background, some distant land of steppe or tundra, inhabited by a more ancient peasantry. When I stopped to admire an apparently home-made hexagonal house somewhere in Erath County, its owner told me that it had once been the municipal bandstand at Thurber ("Don't you know where Thurber is?" he demanded accusatorily)—and instantly in my mind's eye, as we chatted over the fence, I saw the evening band parade in some small garrison town of another age, another longitude, where the bourgeoisie showed off their fineries beneath the streetlights of the square, and bored princes strolled arm-in-arm with visiting nephews from St. Petersburg.

And similar Chekovian sensations repeatedly struck me as I wandered up those silent Texan lanes. All alone sat the postmistress of Duffau, playing dice with herself on a sofa in her now disused store: the room shadowy, and furnished in a kind of transient way, like the back of a removal van—the postmistress mourning the recent loss of "my favorite fishing companion, we'd just go fishing any place together"—the hamlet still and empty in the sunshine outside her door. As for the village of Wizard Wells, once a thriving little spa, it seemed to me like a village forcibly depopulated by Czars or Tartars. Its scattered wooden houses looked all lifeless in the morning, its old health-giving well seemed frozen for ever in time, pitchers still on their hooks, bucket still awaiting its valetudinarians: and when I did find a living inhabitant, he seemed to have awoken from the grave himself, and spoke only, like all the best peasants, of inexplicable happenings long ago—"like there, you see that contraption, that's where we cooked the water—you're meant to cook it, you know, it's stronger that way—before we'd ship it to Oklahoma. . . ."

The longer I wandered, too, the more I was impressed by the aristocratic, almost the imperial style of the great ranches of the countryside.

What archdukes of the West are the terrific Texan pastoralists! Were there ever chateaux more magnificently farmed, more splendidly landscaped, more haughtily aloof than the grandest of these Lazy Ws and Happy Valleys? In them you see the rise of dynasties: as the earls and barons of Europe or Japan emerged to splendor by means of war and plunder, so the lords of Texas clamber to a similar pre-eminence by means of oil and cattle, and celebrate their arrival in just the same ways—with mansions hidden among the trees, with lovely horses and pictures by likely artists, with showy clothes and advantageous marriages and expensively educated daughters—all to be imagined, as one observes the turrets of old castles above Bavarian forests, up the long gravel drives of their immense estates.

Sometimes the foreign allusions are newer—there are no better pizzas in America, I swear it, than the pizzas of the minuscule Italian café recently established by an immigrant chef in Jacksboro—and sometimes they are more direct. The first I saw of Windthorst was the proud tower of its church on a hillock above the interminable plain—a medieval silhouette it seemed, bold against the blazing sun that day, dominating the prosperous farmland of Archer County all around. Windthorst is German through and through, settled by German Catholics in 1891, and is a place of intense corporate personality. The great Benedictine church, which was the focus of the original settlement, is the core of it still, with its school, its convent, and a great grotto of the Virgin Mary, "Our Lady of Highway 281," which was built by the contributions of all those young men of Windthorst who fought in World War II.

Their names are recorded in the church, stout old German names almost without exception, and you can meet them, their sons and their grandsons, any day at Ed's Cafe along the road. Magnificent big men they are, with capable-looking wives and stalwart children—all related to each other it seems, all more than ready for a plate of hash, all talking about swabbers and tornado warnings, all such devoted churchgoers to this day, they told me at Ed's, that every Sunday they have three Masses up at the church (where there is a sound-proof Cry Room, by the way, in which the mothers of the more difficult little Hoffs and Schreibers can listen to the sermon, over the audio system, without disturbing the more hard-of-hearing Ostermanns, Wolfs or Schroeders).

−o / o / o−

The town of George West is named for a Mr. West. The present Mayor of Hamilton is a Mr. Hamilton. Pleasanton is the Birthplace of the Cowboy, Lampasas the Heart of the Cow Country, Blanco the Gem of the Hills, and beside the courthouse at Stephenville a large figure of a cow is labelled MOO-LA! 42 GALLONS ANNUALLY!

Ah, the little towns of Texas, as one by one I passed through them on the long road south—the stately pride of their courthouses, classical or castellated, Georgian or Frenchified, stone, red brick, or in the case of Burnet raw concrete decorated with bas reliefs of pioneering scenes in the Assyrian mode! They greeted me in a regular, almost mathematical succession—some twenty miles between one and the next, as a rule, representing a practical day's journey in the old horse days. I thought them rather like a Texas index, for each had its own particular origins, or its own especial purpose: one an old military base, supervising the wild Indian country to the west, another a market town or a health resort—this one settled by Germans or Norwegians, the next full of Campbells or McTavities—a college here, to generate energy for the place, a refinery or a railroad somewhere else.

And in the course of Texas's headlong rush through history, they have also had their individual ups and downs. Some have been transfigured by strokes of good fortune, like the birth of Lyndon Johnson at Johnson City, or the presence of uranium at Alice (which is the home of the Yawn Motor Company, as it happens, but is very much awake). Some look wistfully back to lost glories: the ex-spa of Mineral Wells, for example, which is dominated still by the enormous but long-vacant Baker Hotel— "Oh," as a wistful resident sighed to me, "the parties we used to have up there, the people who came, Tom Mix and Jean Harlow and I don't know who else!" Some have vanished, like Bridgetown, where nothing is left of a rumbustious past but a few faithful oil-pumps, still bowing incessantly down the generations, and some archaeological kinds of bumps in the ground. And some just seem to meander fatalistically on, like the one, best left nameless, under whose Chamber of Commerce door, all locked up at 2.30 in the afternoon, I slipped a note to say that, alas, I had called for advice about how best to invest ten million in the town, but could not wait. . . .

At Stephenville I went to watch the kids at baseball one evening, and found myself wallowing no less, in the fabled charm of Home Town. It was like a stage show for me, illuminated as it was by the lights of the diamonds, and orchestrated by you-know-what from the radios of cars parked all around. It was as though everyone was acting a part. Small boys burbled authentically here and there, slurping from cans and kicking footballs. Girls shrieked support to boy-friend pitchers, gossipped sibilantly in corners or carried errant babies back to Mom. Young matrons sat in twos or threes talking about clothes and coffee mornings. And beyond the mesh, in that somewhat ghostly light, the young sportsmen played their allotted roles to perfection—the fat freckled one, the tall skinny one, the lovable one who tried so hard, the All-American who never failed—all like figures of a provincial allegory, performing to the smell of popcorn from the snack bar cabin, and the scooting here and there, like insects in and out of the headlights, of exuberant youths on bicycles.

At Three Rivers, I think it was, stopping for a hamburger, I found that I had locked my car keys in the trunk. Small-town Texas swung instantly to my rescue—well, eased itself slowly out of its chairs, tipped its Stetsons over its eyes, strolled into the car-park and stood meditatively eyeing the problem, saying things like "Huh," or "Kindofa problem there." In easy stages they approached the task, sniffing it, feeling it, and when in the end they got the hang of it, enlarged the right aperture, unscrewed the right screws, and found that the keys were not in there at all, since I had left them on the Dairy Queen counter, they seemed not in the least disconcerted, but deftly re-assembling the mechanism, tilting their Stetsons back again, they drifted once more into the café murmuring "You bet, lady, any time."

But the town I liked best of all was Hico. "Why then, you should move right in yourself," suggested the town barber, whom I chanced to meet walking home to his lunch between short-backs-and-sides, and I wouldn't mind. You could do a lot worse than Hico. It does not, perhaps, look anything very special—just the classic American huddle of houses around an intersection, where State Highways 6 and 220 join US 281: built of brick mainly, I think, with overlays of clapboard, with the usual suggestion of wasteland at one edge, where the railroad used to run, and a hint of suburbia in the comfortable gardened houses away from the highway, towards one of which, as it happens, the barber was making his way that day. But there are green trees speckling the town all over, and cheerful weathered faces in the streets, and an air of family comradeship laced with a proper ration of gossip.

Yes, you could do a lot worse than Hico. In Hico (pronounced Hy-co, they told me, if you're sober, Hicko if you're drunk) you can have your car washed by Junior High School pupils next Saturday in the park. In Hico you can get your hair done at Chat-'n-Curl prior to the Friday Nite Special Catfish Buffet. In Hico the Hico Meat Company will Process your Deer for you, the motel is OWNED BY TEXANS, and at the drugstore you are welcome to pick up a complimentary copy of the Ladies' Almanac. In Hico Firemen Only Are Allowed On Fire Trucks.

I am half a Hican already. See that figure down there by the Bosque River, way down by the willows, this side the bridge, chewing hickory-smoked jerky and reading the social intelligence in the *Hico News Review?* Yeah, that's me.

–o / o / o–

"What do I do?" said a man in the Koffee Kup Kafe, "I don't do nothin'. What does he do? He don't do nothin' either. We're all retarded here."

I was going for a walk along the river at Lampasas one evening when three motorcyclists approached me very slowly in line ahead. They were all tremendously old, and absolutely identical. They wore jaunty baseball caps, but beneath the peaks their faces were hide-like, like the faces of tortoises: and as they passed me, one by one those visages momentarily split, with a "Hi," or a "Hi there," before sealing themselves once more into leatheriness.

They were like visitors from another world, or from some Unidentified Retirement Object, and there were times indeed as I travelled through Texas when I thought that the Aged were about to take over the State. It is true of course that in most parts of the Western world the old are coming into their inheritance, assisted by greater affluence, greater leisure and the vagaries of the birth-rate, but I never observed the phenomenon more vividly than I did along 281. Whole towns seemed to be seized already. Whole counties were occupied by squadrons of Kamping Koaches, encampments of Mobile Homes, and cult-like images of geriatry haunted me everywhere. Through the big windows of the CIA Retirement Club at Wichita Falls I saw them, I saw them, conspiring there in their eye-shades over the card tables. At the Crazy Woman Hotel at Mineral Falls

I found them already in possession, for it had been turned into a retirement home, and a notice above the reception desk ominously warned me:

If you must spit be sure to spit
Some place else than where I sit.

Almost anywhere along 281, if you go down to the town camper park
in the evening, you will find the old folk plotting their next move,
crouched beneath the awnings of their Recreational Vehicles beneath
dim lights over paper cups of stimulant, like tank commanders in the
field. . . .

Actually in the rural reaches of north and central Texas the Senior
Citizens are mostly survivors. They are representatives of a less aggressive
army—the rural rearguard, still entrenched in the countryside they were
born to, as all around them youth, hope and opportunity hasten by to the
big cities. All along 281, as along countless other highways in every continent, one feels the pull of metropolitan life, like some massive unseen
magnet over the horizon. In England I sometimes feel the whole island
is tilted imperceptibly in the direction of London; in India a whole race,
a whole sub-continent often seems on its way to Calcutta or Bombay; in
Texas Fort Worth, Dallas, Austin, Houston, San Antonio are always
present in the idea of them, however remote they may be on the map.
For the most part US 281 avoids the big towns, but all along the way
their names crop up on the road signs like come-on signals—come over
here to Big D, next left for the lights of Cowtown, Taste the Good Life
in Your Capital City!

So the young move on, where the action is and the jobs are, and the
survivors linger on in a countryside that sometimes seems almost as
empty as it was in the days when Texas first began. It is oddly like history running backwards. I actually noticed the absence of the young—
visually, I mean, as one might notice a lack of streetlamps, or motor-
cycles. All too often the dancehalls and saloons of 281 have long been
boarded-up, offering only spectral shades of yesterday's honky-tonk.
"Run out of kiddos!" I was told in Antelope, when I asked why the
school had been turned into a community center, and when Mrs. Effie
cork of Hamilton County demonstrated to me on her own front porch
how to make a poke bonnet, I felt I was in direct living contact with the
Texas that was there before the young were born.

On the other hand down in the warm south, where the land softens and palms itself into the valley of the Rio Grande, age really is on the march. Down there young people still abound, in the prosperous market-garden country of the valley, but the place has been invaded by old folk from elsewhere. Go South, Old Man! "Welcome Winter Texans," says a sign outside Edinburg, "Valley Folk Are Glad You're Here," and it seems a prudent attitude to me: for there mile after mile the Adult Retirement Homes extend, powerfully affecting the whole nature of the country, swarmed in and out of by vigorous elderly denizens on their daily forays to garage sales and flea markets. "We're all retarded here," said the man in the Koffee Kup Cafe, but he said it grimly tongue-in-cheek.

And if you have a taste for the symbolisms of age, how about the retired couple I found mowing the grass at Lynn Creek cemetery near Jacksboro? This lonely little garden, having long outlived the communities it once served, is a *memento mori* in every way: elegiac winds blow through its cedars and live oaks, memorial irises blossom wild among its tombs, and Texan clans lie in their generations all around. My Senior Citizens were mowing it for the first time, having just undertaken the contract, and were finding it heavy going. As the husband said, "it takes a million turns in and out the gravestones—I only hope I don't fall right in one of the graves myself!" I laughed rather hollowly at the quip, as the breeze stirred the leaves above my head, but later took the opportunity, when they kindly allowed it, of mowing a few square feet of grass myself. It is not everyone who has mown a Texan graveyard: besides, if you can't beat them. . . .

– o / o / o –

Halfway through my journey, rather more than 300 miles south of Red River, I passed tangentially through the delectable hill and lake country west of Austin, where the rich scudded around in motorboats visiting each other in luxurious lake-side condominiums, and the village stores had turned themselves into delicatessens and were selling Earl Grey tea and Rumanian canned rhubarb. But hardly had I emerged from that happy Shangri-La when I entered another sort of hallucination, for I arrived at San Antonio in the middle of its annual Fiesta. Generally speaking, I am told, San Antonio is a reasonably down-to-earth working town, the third largest in Texas and some say the nicest: but the night I arrived was the night of the great water-parade along the San Antonio

river, meandering through its artificial canyon among the downtown
buildings: and so, falling into the hands of hospitable San Antonians, I
was ushered into a dream.

What phantasmagoric gulley was that stream beneath our windows,
lined along its curling course with what inconceivable multitudes? What
shapes were those on the water passing by, those drifting baubles of light
and color, those gesticulating figures weirdly dressed? Whose flags were
these, thick across every street, and what manner of people, these sombre
men with Mickey Mouse balloons? From what exotic divisions did these
generals come, with their massed medals of unrecognizable campaigns,
their drooping epaulettes and their theatrically gilded caps?

The talk in that town seemed a kind of gibberish to me, of Ugly Kings
and Fauberge Courts, of Cavaliers and Coronations, of curtseying instructions and 60,000 dresses. The whole city seemed seized in an arcane
ecstasy all its own, jumping up and down with the excitement of it, discussing nothing else. We dined at a club which, with its great white
portico among the palm trees, seemed to have been transported there
from Calcutta, and as we walked across the lawn at the end of the day
we saw a great grey armadillo, itself like some beast of the imagination,
scuttling through the half-light into the shrubbery.

−o / o / o−

"My statement," an artist told me in Stephenville, "is that we're all goin'
to die out one day"—and he pointed to a forlorn sort of bird-object, made
of feathers, wire and pampas grass, hanging from the ceiling and entitled,
if I heard him right, "The Last Mating." "That's my statement."

The last Texan mating seemed a long way off to me, but still it is true
that Texas and war, if not Texas and Armageddon, rather go together.
Everywhere down 281, itself designated the American Legion Memorial
Highway, I heard the rumors of old conflicts, because for years this old
cattle trail passed dangerously close to the Indian country of the west. It
was, I suppose, a Hell Fire Alley of long ago, and from its forts and encampments the military made their reconnaissances and forays into the
territories of the Apaches, the Comanches or the Wichitas. It looks like
fighting country still, with its hidden gullies for ambushes, its crests for
warriors to silhouette themselves upon: and even now, if you put your
mind to it, and look away to the west over these silent prairies, you may
imagine the smoke of the tribes rising on those horizons.

The mementos of the Indian wars are vivid still in these parts. Here was a massacre, here an abduction, here for the first time an Indian was tried in a white man's court, and here at Burnet soldiers and Comanches fought a bloody battle in the eerie pitch-black of a cave! Once I noticed an old dirt track running east to west across my route, and thought it a somehow epic look: I was right, for it turned out to be the Marcy Trail, by which the Texas Rangers travelled to their outposts on the remotest frontier of the day—a strategic highway straight as a die still, still heroically rutted, from limit to limit of my vision.

Nor were they only Indian enemies, that the folk-memory of 281 recalled for me. Think of it! As recently as 1915 infantry was on guard to protect the King Ranch against Mexican raiders! And when at Windthorst I spoke thoughtlessly of "the last war," meaning as Europeans do World War II, they looked at me a little sadly: 91 of their young men, out of a total population of 409, fought in Korea and Vietnam. No wonder Texas has a military air. Even now half the towns down my road seem to have their military bases. Fighters zip now and then across your line of sight; soldiers in fatigues tumble out of trucks into a Jack-in-a-Box cafés; Fort Hood, the city of Lampasas proudly tells you, is "the biggest military base in the Free World."

The central shrine of my journey, as of Texas itself, was the Alamo. I happened to get there on the day of its annual pilgrimage, and the military virtues were certainly paramount then. White-scarved soldiers of the Old Guard stood statuesque behind the dais, colonels in dark glasses were everywhere, American Legionnaires were in attendance, bands played, ribbons blazed, a general assured us (ambiguously, I thought, since all its heroes died) that the story of the Alamo showed us what it meant to be an American, and most formidably of all, the Daughters of the Texas Republic themselves, shock troops with a vengeance, were in parade in full front-line regalia of pearls and Neiman-Marcus hats.

For me it all came more disturbingly to a head, though, at Harlinge, in the south: for there on a former air base two of the most relentlessly military institutions in America live cheek-by-jowl in machismo, presided over gigantically by the original plaster cast of the Iwo Jima Memorial. To one of pacifist leanings this is a daunting place. You come first to the Marine Military Academy, described variously as "the toughest prep school in the world" and "a vanguard against terrorism," whose

boys are educated to the sternest precepts of the U.S. Marine Corps and
whose teachers are former Marines themselves. Slogans of Free Enterprise, Traditional Morality, Discipline and Respect resound through this
forbidding campus; the pupils live in barracks blocks and are kept up to
the mark by retired Marine Corps drill instructors. Ronald Reagan, after
a visit once, told some satisfied parents (Mr. and Mrs. Gene Snuggs,
actually, of Snuggs Diversified Investments) that it gave him "a new
sense of security about the future of our country"; but my own heart
sank, as I tried to imagine leaving a child of mine, smiling goodbye
through his tears no doubt, and possibly clutching his teddy-bear, in the
care of General Spanjer and his sergeant-majors.

But there is worse up the road, for there the self-styled colonels of the
Confederate Air Force have turned the idea of war and all its squalors
into a species of celebration. There on the tarmac stand the hideous
bombers of World War II, preserved not in loathing, but in love; there
in the museum are the guns, bombs, torpedoes and battle-plans that cost
the world so many million lives, presided over by kindly local ladies, and
offered as "a warm and exciting step back into yesteryear." It is also, they
claim, "an injection of uncut inspiration all of us could use from time to
time": but I distrusted its pretensions from the start, and detested its
gung-ho enthusiasm. I think they love it all. Outside the Operations
Room a place is permanently reserved for the aircraft of the CAF's commanding officer, Colonel Jethro E. Culpeper, who is described as having
fought in all branches of the U.S. armed forces in every theatre of action
throughout World War II: but I was glad to find that this gentleman was
only mythical, or we might have got into an argument.

– o / o / o –

*Now, I have some news for you ranchers of Texas. The Hereford bull,
who comes originally from my own part of the world, does not pronounce
himself Hearford, as you seem to suppose, but Herreford. "Is that right?
Well, he pronounces himself Hearford on my ranch."*

Hunched, purposeful, tingling with energy, a Santa Gertrudis bull
glowered at me over the fence of the King Ranch, but only briefly, for he
had better things to do. He was preparing himself for lust. By striking
the ground savagely with his front hoof, he was throwing dirt all over
himself, and with each shower of soil he made a kind of grunt, a muted
bellow, louder with each successive lunge, until at last he felt himself

ready: and shaking his great head without another glance at me, off he loped tremendously towards his apprehensive herd.

The fauna of Texas is a mighty pageant, from the twitchy long-tailed birds of the telegraph wires to such noble ruffians of the range. I watched coots swim through bayou weeds, I saw deer bounce across shrublands, I mourned the passing of a hundred squashed oppossums, I marvelled at the grace of the quarter-horse, I heard tales of coyotes and wild cats, I lay in wait for jack-rabbits, I saw an armadillo at the Argylle Club. You cannot escape the Texan bestiary. When I stopped by at McDonald's Food Store near Lampasas to buy a carton of milk, Mr. McDonald asked me if I would care to buy a horse at the same time.

Earthiness is a Texan grace—some might say a saving grace. If it sometimes expresses itself in crudity, it also reveals a closeness to things original and organic that you would never feel in California, say, even among the healthiest of health-food farmers, or even I think in the great farmlands of the wheat belt. It is true that all too many beasts of Texas are destined for the slaughter-house, raised for profit, killed for cash, but still one feels in this state, more than in most places, some old working partnership with the rest of God's creatures: a rough-and-ready, take-it-or-leave-it, but essentially honest sort of relationship, as frank in the abbatoir as it is in the stables.

So all down 281 I made the acquaintance of animals. The most enchanting ones I saw were the livestock of a goat ranch near Edinburg. They were not all goats, for the woman who runs 4H has a magnetic empathy with animals of all sorts, and is surrounded by them always. Ponies and cattle nibble affectionately at her feet, border collies bark gaily at her coming, peacocks preen their feathers for her, hens flutter their wings, little black cats jump upon her shoulders, nanny-goats line up to be milked. She and her husband live in a trailer, half-concealed by tall cacti, and all around them down the years the creatures prance, skip and lactate their loyalty.

The most moving animal I saw was a white lamb in a kennel at the mission of San Francisco de la Espada, outside San Antonio, for he was a living emblem of Texan continuity. There has been a mission here for 250 years, a little church beside a tree-specked plaza, a school, a mossy frondy aqueduct, scattered houses all around and families descended to this day from the Spaniards and Indians of the original settlement. And that lamb, too, has always been there, if only figuratively, for this is the mission of St. Francis, and now as always, they told me at the rectory, animals are a very part of the place—the lamb in his kennel, Augustine the cat, two white doves in a cage in the sunshine, and a little mongrel dog who, scratching himself out in the middle of the plaza, must surely have been here in one incarnation or another since the Fathers first arrived.

And the animals I admired most I saw in the open range one stormy day when the sun was black with thundercloud and hailstones were beginning to slap upon my windscreen. I looked to my left as I braced myself for the tempest, and there advancing across the scrub, illuminated marvellously now by flashes of lightning, and swirled about by the vapor rising from the warm ground, a team of Angora goats was on the move, heads down, muscles taut, and led by a fine old bearded patriarch, all raunch and guts, who seemed to me the very image of Old Texas, two- or four-legged as you please.

$$-o\,/\,o\,/\,o-$$

Me: Where are you from?

Hotel maid: I'm not from nowhere, I'm from Mexico.

The Hispanicity of Texas did not strike me much at first—a Tex Mex restaurant here and there, a few bilingual signs, snatches of mariachis. But as I went south, gradually I felt the complexion of the place changing: not just the skin complexion, but the complexion of life itself, the pace and temper of it. As in some flickering old movie, I seemed to see Texas changing its character before my eyes, as the ethnic balance shifted, until down in the southern counties, Wilson, Live Oak or Jim Wells, small dark ladies in enormous limousines seemed to be shooting into 281 at every intersection, hypnotically beautiful black-eyed babies gazed at me in grocery stores, and half the people I inquired the way of seemed to know the neighborhood rather less intimately than I did myself. It is true that in the course of my journey I passed through nine degrees of latitude—from 34 to 26, about like going from Berlin to the French Riviera: even so, this transformation of temperament and appearance took me rather by surprise.

At a small town called Evant, well to the north, I first heard the whisper of a Mexican Issue. There, spying an enclave that looked to me beguilingly like a gypsy encampment, all scampering animals, discarded bedsteads and tumble-down huts, I inquired of a neighboring resident who it was that lived there. "Mexicans, that's who," she said. "This town used to be all white, no colored people, no nothing. Then those Mexicans moved in." She did not say it unkindly exactly, only cautiously, and indeed they did not seem to have moved in very far—an ethnic nibble, no more, on the fringe of the little town. But by the time I reached San Antonio the matter lay more thickly on the air. This has always been a Spanish city, once the capital of Spanish Texas indeed, but it is getting more Spanish every day—so Spanish already indeed that it often seemed to me more like a South American than a North American city. Old undercurrents of resentment sharpened the edge of that tumultuous fiesta, and conversations were full of ethnic allusion and innuendo. Everybody talked to me about illegal immigration, about indentured labor, about border-guard bribes and sweat-shop wages: and here as so often in contemporary America, all around me I felt the growing power of the Spanish-speaking people, the pulse of their music, the flow of their tongue, the revival perhaps of their pride.

Of course Texas itself is very Spanishy. Spaniards founded it, Spaniards named it, Spanish words, customs, foods and artifacts are part of its everyday fabric. The very style of the state speaks, if only obliquely, of conquistadores and grandees. But it is a new kind of Hispanicization that is changing it now—not the grand Castilian kind, or the dashing cowboy kind, but something different out of Mexico—the Spanishness above all of poor, troubled or angry people, who have nothing much to lose, and who have come to the United States, I sometimes speculate, as much in resentment as in hope.

They are making a new Texas, I think. Indeed by the time I got to the Rio Grande Valley I felt I was hardly in Texas at all, or at least only in some heavily mutated version of the Lone Star State we know and love. Gone, I felt, was its easy grandeur of heritage and purpose. Three parallel thoroughfares run through the Valley from McAllen to Brownsville. In the north is Expressway 82, all speed and exit signs. In the middle is Business Route 82, all trailer havens, business malls and First National Banks—42 miles of Main Street, they like to call it down there. In the south is my own 281, running hangdog and outclassed now through the wide fields of fruit and vegetables, beneath the spindly palms, saluted only along the way by listless Hispanic villages and direction signs to Mexico. And to the south again is the Rio Grande itself, where the wetbacks wade, where the socialites of San Antonio get their housemaids, where the vegetable packers get their cheap labor, and the border patrols keep their ceaseless but less than incorruptible watch.

It is like a topographical allegory—those four parallel lines upon the map, each expressing a different origin, a different intention, a different style. Fields of tension seemed to me to lie between them all, giving the whole Valley, for all its warmth and color, some indefinable air of bitterness or suspicion. It is no longer a very beautiful vale. The early travellers thought it a kind of paradise, with its richness of foliage, its benign climate and its miraculously fertile soil: but it has long since been tarnished by the developers, and looks today more a Limbo than an Elysium. Still, it does remain undeniably exotic, a kind of Texas Riviera beneath those avenues of palms, and this makes its nuances of conflict all the more disturbing. Sometimes it seemed to me that the houses of the richer residents, encouched in sprinkled lawns and jacaranda, were like the homes of colonial settlers in some sub-tropical empire: and when a notice warned me that I was entering a Tick Eradication Zone, as I drove through the potato fields, I was reminded obscurely of no-man's-lands and neutral zones, where misunderstanding armies eye each other across the wire, wondering what will happen next.

Before I left the Valley I paid a visit to the Shrine of the Virgin at San Juan, one of the holiest places of Mexican Catholicism in the United States. I thought it might soothe me, and indeed there was a profound sanctity to the great modern church, its massed displays of grateful votaries, the discarded crutches of its faithful cured and the beloved figure of the Madonna itself, high on the eastern wall. But the longer I watched those Mexican families at their devotions, the less serene I felt. Anxiety was writ upon those kind fathers' faces, sacrifice upon the features of their wives, and the little children kneeling at the rail, so reverent, so hushed, looked all too poignantly like lambs for the world's slaughter.

—o / o / o—

"If you don't like the weather, wait a minute": Old Texan Saying, repeated to me twice a day for three weeks.

Rain and sun, dry and wet, all the way through Texas the weather had been mocking me, shifting my mood from day to day and doubtless warping my perceptions. But though the sun shone brightly on me when I arrived in Brownsville, where 281 finally deposits its travellers upon the

International Bridge to Mexico, and though it was proper to end such a journey upon a frontier line, still I found myself a little melancholy.

Brownsville is hardly the best of Texas, being at once tumultuous of motion and hangdog of manner. It reminds me of several other towns— Port Said, Panama, Trieste—where cultures are tossed against each other by history, now one pre-eminent, now another, but it somehow lacks the sting or fizz of confrontation. Its shapes and symptoms are threadbare, or exhausting: bazaar-like shops of china and cheap toys, humped scurrying figures loaded with tote bags and brown paper parcels, hooting horns, bumpy tarmac, lines of cars at border posts. Only a certain sad excitement attends the bridge itself, with all its mixed emotions—this is after all one of the supreme boundaries of the world, the boundary between the richest society ever established, and the world of poverty, frustration, ill-health and ignorance which, starting just over there in Mexico, extends in so ominous a swathe from here to Bangladesh.

These were not the sensations I wanted of the Lone Star State. In Brownsville's graceless streets my Texas, which had begun at Red River with so exuberant a bang, went out at the Rio Grande not even with a whimper, only a half-hearted haggle. I was homesick already. Where was Ed's Cafe now? I asked myself rhetorically as I looked over the brown and sluggish river. Where did Brownsville's bluebonnets nod? Where was the barber of Hico, where the postmistress of Duffau? To whom would I turn in this unlovely town, if I left my keys in the trunk? So I gave my car in at the airport and took a ticket northwards once again, humming to myself as I boarded the aircraft a lyric I had lately grown to like, to the effect that good ol' boys is all we'll ever be.

The Best of Everything

STOCKHOLM, SWEDEN

On Sunday evening in summer the week-end sailors of Stockholm come streaming home from their sailing grounds in the Baltic peninsula—from Vaxholm and Grinda, from Gällnö and Djurö and Möja, where the island-jumbled waters of the Swedish coast debouch into the open sea. The sun is glinting then on the golden baubles that ornament the towers and steeples of their city; flags fly bravely from masts and rooftops; and the small boats hasten sun-bleached and purposeful through the harbor, bronzed fathers at the helm, tousled children flat on the deck, like the ships of a light flotilla returning from distant action.

Into the Slussen lock the boats jam themselves, watched by the lock-keeper in his glass cabin (TV monitor flickering in its shadows), and with a ponderous movement of steel gates, a swoosh and dripping of water, they are raised from the level of the sea to the level of the lake that lies beyond; and so they disperse into the gathering dusk, away among the myriad creeks of the city, to nose their way into unsuspected canals between the apartment blocks, to tie up at private jetties among the trees, or to disappear into the numberless marinas that lie concealed, like so many little naval bases, all over the watery capital.

War-like similes come naturally when one writes about the spectacle. It is as though those yachting bankers and navigational shopkeepers, those sea-going secretaries of Stockholm, are retreating once again into their own private fastness, clanging the lock-gates behind them against all comers, to lie low within their city limits until the next week-end. Stockholm was founded as a fortress, and its heart is like a fortress still, for standing guard to this day above that lock is the tight, tough island quarter called Gamla Stan, Old Town, the original nucleus of the city, whose churches and tall houses stand jammed together cap-à-pie and whose silhouette, at the exact place where the saltwater of the Baltic Sea shifts to the fresh of the Swedish hinterland, is a sort of masonry defiance.

When those bright yachts and launches vanish into the mass of the city, though, their helmsmen are not escaping from any tangible enemy. They are merely taking allegorical refuge against the world's bad luck, retreating behind the breakwaters that have enabled them, for several generations, to enjoy a nicely balanced extract of the best of everything.

– o / o / o –

They have created for themselves, all in all, the most beautiful capital in Europe, but its beauty is spare, not lavish. In Stockholm's outdoor folk museum you may see how simply the people of these parts lived not so long ago, and realize how suddenly, by European standards, this city's sophistication arrived. There the bare island rock still shows among the farmsteads, the wood smoke rises scented from the hearth, sheep bleat and reindeer lope; but it does not feel particularly remote from the life of the city all about, and the Stockholmers in jeans and sunglasses, out for the afternoon, hanging over the goat pen or wandering through the roughhewn wooden buildings, do not look especially anachronistic. Although there have been people living in Gamla Stan for 700 years, nothing in Stockholm feels very antique; and this queer osmosis of the ages, medieval and modern apparently contemporaneous, gives the metropolis a curiously contrived air, and makes it rather like an invented city, started from scratch and put together as a unit.

Take the shape of it. This is all planners' logic, whether thirteenth or twentieth century. Slap in the middle stands Gamla Stan, like a toy town on an island, and there even now Sweden's offices of national consequence are concentrated: Parliament, the Swedish Academy, the Ombudsman's office, the Stock Exchange, the old royal palace. Then to the north across the bridges, the city's own institutions are conveniently disposed: city hall and opera house, galleries and museums, banks and corporate offices, hotels and railway stations and downtown shopping center. There is a pleasure island to the east, with a fun fair on it; there is a diplomatic quarter; to the south is the big island of Södermalm, where artists, political activists and dropouts are alleged to live; and all around the outer city, encouched in greenery and ring roads, are the high-rise suburbs, satellites and garden cities of the Swedish workers' paradise.

And sure enough, as in some living exhibition, in all these districts the inhabitants are to be observed meticulously honoring their categories. Unmistakable stockbrokers eat their luncheons in the tall open windows of the Stock Exchange dining room. Obvious magnates step from metallically painted turbo-limousines into metallically sheathed corporate headquarters. Resplendent cavalrymen, all brass and bobbled helmets, labor up the cobbled roadway for the changing of the guard at the palace. Musicians in eighteenth-century costumes are revealed shaking the spittle from their flutes in the back quarters of concert rooms. And in half an hour on Södermalm recently I introduced myself to a writer working on a masterpiece in a park, exchanged views with a Trotskyite animal liberationist, and was accosted by a pair of genial prickly layabouts in a cemetery.

Then there is the absoluteness of everything. Everything is absolutely so. Surely no organically developing city ever produced an Old Town so utterly Old Town as Gamla Stan, where the gabled mansions of Hanseatic merchants look down on cobbled lanes and courtyards, where student guitarists play laments outside picturesque taverns, and where in the center of everything the Storkyrkan, Stockholm's cathedral, is a very prodigy of theatrical baroque, all cherubs, tassels, trumpets, garlands, painted draperies and mighty gilded organ. No city hall was ever quite so civic as Stockholm's, either; no Grand Hotel ever grander; no opera house much more operatic, especially when the flambeaux blaze above its famous restaurant; and certainly no underground railway could be more frankly subterranean than the new Hjulsta line, whose walls are of rough bare rock, decorated with grotto-like paintings and sculptures, and whose stations are warmed only by the exhalations of its passengers.

−o / o / o−

All this is as if a group of Scandinavian planners, sitting in a revolving restaurant on top of an observation tower, had mapped out their city rationale over pickled herrings and a temperate allowance of aquavit.

There are aspects of Stockholm, though, that also possess elements of mystery. Its setting is distinctly exotic, among those wooded isles and waters. Its climate, in sunshine as in snow, is marvellously suggestive of tundra or northern waste. Sometimes, when a fierce wind blows out of the north, the faces of the scurrying citizens, drawn tight by the bluster of it, all seem to acquire a Lappish look, their eyes rather slanted, their cheekbones heightened, their skulls apparently narrowed, until they too, tending as they often do anyway toward an ideal androgyny, seem like a species devised especially for the setting by fablers or geneticists.

And what terrific enigmas of Stockholm history baffle the visiting innocent! To the average outsider this city's past is as remote as troll lore or neolithic surmise, its heroes and villains like figures of fantasy, its denouements blurred but evidently thrilling. Even its one epic period, those decades of the seventeenth century when Sweden was a great power, and Stockholm an imperial capital—even those classic years of splendor are obscure enough to most of us. Yet more than anything the memory of them dictates the city's style to this day, and casts its refulgence over the whole immense invention.

This is paradoxical, for it is a patrician allure, dead and gone long since, only its shadow surviving in a city of triumphant bourgeois functionalism. It lingers symbolically in purely ornamental functions of the Swedish monarchy: it lingers theatrically in Riddarholm Church, Stockholm's anteroom to Valhalla, where kings lie beneath gigantic sarcophagi in huge gloomy chapels, and marshals more generally forgotten are immortalized in the crests and cartouches of invariable victory. And it survives most hauntingly of all in the hulk of the seventeenth-century warship *Wasa*, pride of the Swedish navy in its most prideful epoch, which capsized within sight of the city on her maiden voyage, but was salvaged in 1961. The *Wasa* is presently housed in a structure like an enormous oxygen tent, maintained for preservation purposes in the constant state of high humidity. This makes an inspection of her remains a disturbingly awful experience, like visiting an ancient queen in a coma. Tremendously she lies there, tremendously Swedish, and recondite carved figures glare at you from her gunwales, and monsters sneer at you from her prow, and huge devices of power and authority loom there through the heat; and the hot, damp, sickroom air makes you feel she really is some living creature, sustained only by scientific support systems, but sentient still in all her age and tragedy.

−*o* / *o* / *o*−

In the big open arena that has been scooped out of the city's new commercial center, beneath the Kulturhuset and the glass pillar of Sergels
Torg, a group of singers is performing a children's song, and encouraging
its audience to participate. "Come along now," the leader cries, "arms in
air, touch your toes, hands up high, and plunk your cheek when the
drum goes bang." The audience by and large responds half-heartedly,
but at the back of the crowd a solitary middle-aged citizen, placing his
briefcase on the ground, solemnly conforms. Obediently he stretches his
arms, diligently he tries to touch his toes, and when the drumbeat sounds,
pop! resonantly he plunks his cheek out with his finger.

Doth not a Swede bleed? Many of the well-known Stockholm stereo-
types are true, but many are false. The charm of this place is not entirely
bland, as reputation has it, and its citizens are not all numbed by success,
neutrality and social security. They are only human, like the rest of us.
They leave litter about sometimes, and scrawl graffiti in subway trains.
Argumentative drunks get picked up by gum-chewing cops, here as
everywhere. Prostitutes signal their services from the doorways of Brunke-
bergstorg, and circling Saabs respond. Stockholmers are not perfect. It is
just that, like everything else in their ageless city, they seem somehow to
lack the bumps, the scratches, and the wrinkles of normal evolution.

This is alienation of a kind, as Sweden's critics always claim, but if
there is pathos to it, there is also comfort, for in their smooth and man-
nered uniformity the Stockholmers present to the world at large a remarkably club-like or familial image. In the summer evenings the public park
called Kungstradgarden is transformed into a free entertainment center
for the citizenry, and though there are always foreign tourists about, and
Finns, and Turkish immigrants, still a powerful sense of community pre-
vails. The young people who sway and scream to the rock bands all seem
to know each other; the dancers who waltz to the accordion trio exchange smiles in a neighborly way; the two old men at the giant chess-
board, the one with a pipe, the other with an umbrella, look as though
they have been playing together all their lives, so comradely are their
grunts and silences, so fraternal the mock salutes or stagy groans with
which they greet each other's successes.

Stockholm seems to be a city of particularly strong affinities or en-
claves—young with young, vegetarians with vegetarians, Finn with

Finn—giving it the air of a whole conglomeration of semiprivate associations, all linked by common membership of the capital itself. Everywhere across the summer city, on platforms at the water's edge, on the high cliff terraces of Södermalm, canopied in the lush green of city parks or jammed in the shadowy alleys of the Old Town, cafés give the impression of being occupied exclusively by their own habitués. In the evening the couples standing in line to get into the Victoria Restaurant look, at a glance, not merely like so many brothers, sisters, or cousins, but actually like so many clones. Even in the criminal courts, judge, assessors, prosecutor and accused face each other across the circumstances in familiar equality, open-necked or short-sleeved every one, and the prisoner swings back and forth in his comfortable swivel chair like a showbiz guest on a talk show.

In theory, at least, all Stockholmers have a say in the running and the development of their city, and this is lucky, for although they have escaped all our wars and the worst of our depressions, they have experienced in the past decade a trauma of urban renewal. As though in penance for never having been bombed, the planners tore down the whole of the commercial center anyway and built it up again in the very latest mode, levelling its bulges and resolving its quirks. Like members of a family, Stockholmers still mourn the loss of so many homely streets and familiar corners, shops their grandmothers always recommended, theaters they knew from childhood Christmasses; but as a family adjusts to a new in-law or a coming of age, so they are accustoming themselves to their angular new downtown, which suggests to me a formal exercise in capitalist realism, but which already seems about as old, or about as new, as Gamla Stan itself.

–o / o / o–

Stockholm is not a particularly quiet city. Bridges reverberate; trains rumble over the lake; bands play in parks and palace yard, itinerant musicians in side streets; and ever and again the excursion boats hoot their whistles—sometimes, like the venerable steamship *Drottningholm* when she is in a particular hurry to sail, in a Strauss-like rhythm, oom-pah-pah, oom-pah-pah, before, with a scurry of propellers and a cloud of white steam, she reverses from the quay. Occasionally, however, perhaps when you are in the lee of the wind, a peculiar hush seems to overcome the city, and then all that passing traffic, all those hurrying crowds, all the busy craft and flapping flags seem reduced to silent motion, as though the inventors of the place, when they programmed it, built into it the capacity, now and then, to switch the sound off.

In those muted moments especially, Stockholm seems above all a city of the water: on one side of Gamla Stan the sea, the way to Russia; on the other side Lake Malaren, extending a hundred miles into the heart of Sweden. The pale of the water, the cool of the water, above all, perhaps, its sheltering quality, pervade the idioms of the city, and the ships that are everywhere still seem Stockholm's most natural means of locomotion: tall-funneled white ferries chugging here and there, icebreakers waiting for the winter, barges and fishing boats and old schooners moored in their scores along Strandvagen and the Södermalm quays, yachts and motorboats never out of sight, country steamers setting off for the island towns of the archipelago, and sometimes a pair of the Swedish navy's torpedo boats scudding into town with their long-haired conscripts like medieval seamen at the rails.

Far up its Baltic cove Stockholm sits beside its waters safe and snug. Sometimes I like to sit looking out across the harbor from a bench in Kungstradgarden, beside the statue of Charles XII the invader of Russia (who waves his sword in a peremptory manner, as it happens, in the general direction of Leningrad). This makes me feel like a defector: not from any particular ideology, or any particular State indeed, but rather from everywhere else, all other societies. All around me foreigners of many kinds are sitting defector-like too: aging refugees from the Vietnam draft I dare say, dissident poets from Estonia, Kurds (who maintain a cultural center in Södermalm), Armenians (who are said to plot outrages here), fretful Pakistanis or resentful Palestinians.

In such moods, indeed, it sometimes seems to me that the Stockholmers themselves are one and all defectors too, withdrawn as they are from so many of the world's preoccupations. Certainly they have some of the introspective melancholy of refugees, as well as the esprit de corps: like exiles in their own city, clinging together yet half yearning for somewhere else. They are a reserved and cautious citizenry still, and carefree spontaneity is not their forte. In theory they admire unconventionality, but in practice they are less than wild: even the punkers are moderate punkers, and the swingers of the Stockholm discos look like unusually restrained young Californians of the 1960s. When I once tried to demonstrate to a cabdriver, in mime, my desire to visit the law courts, my preposterous antics upon the city pavement—humbly kneeling to portray the accused, sagely grimacing to impersonate the judge—cut no ice at all: nobody smiled, nobody shouted recognition, and all around me the Stockholmers watched in chaste bemusement.

This steady aloofness sets the seal upon the synthetic feel of Stockholm. No proletarian banter jollies this city along. No merry Berliners chaff at you, no salty Brooklynese sounds across these market stalls. Only those pale blue Stockholm eyes contemplatively assess your situation, and those reasonable Stockholm voices, kind and patient, explain the facts of life. It is like being under an anesthetic, or rather, perhaps, waking up from one, and discovering there, imprecisely through your developing awareness, the clean masked faces of the nurses, eyes on the cardiac reading, fingers deftly at your pulse, voices murmuring textbook reassurances.

−o / o / o−

It makes you feel lonely—not for yourself, because you are soon going home—but for your comforters. They must stay behind, masked against germs perpetually. Luckier though they are than all the rest of us, there is to the Stockholmers a wistful suggestion of exclusion, even rejection, for by the nature of things they stand on the edge of the world, always looking in.

Not that those yachtsmen, hastening home through Slussen on a Sunday evening, look in the least wistful. They look rich, healthy, and pleased with life. All the same, sometimes one sees a larger vessel gliding the other way in the evening, heading eastward for the open sea; and as the setting sun catches the hammer and sickle upon her funnel, and her white form disappears behind the wooded heights of Djurgarden, whatever your views, whatever your fears or sympathies, some frisson may shiver your spine as you watch her go, to wonder at the great and terrible destination she is heading for, out of this fine free city of common sense, through the pleasant islands of its archipelago.

In Ruritania

CETINJE, YUGOSLAVIA

There is only one proper way to go to Cetinje. You start at the Gulf
of Kotor, the spectacular mountain-ringed fjord that disrupts the
coastline of southern Yugoslavia near the Albanian frontier, and you take
the hair-raising spiral road, what used to be called the Ladder of Cattaro,
up what appears at first sight to be the sheer face of a mountain—high,
high up the formidable rock rampart that rings the heart of Montenegro.
For many centuries people have come this way with trepidation: on
mules, frightened of bandits; on cavalry horses, terrified of guerrillas; in
troop carriers, wary of partisans; and now in tourist coaches and rented
cars, heart-in-mouth at the prospect of having a blowout and falling off
the edge. Probably no road on earth travels so far so shortly. It is only a
few miles from the bottom of the Ladder to the top, but in the course of
its fifteen loops you change worlds. At the bottom is the Mediterranean
world—towers and villas the Venetians built, cruise ships from Piraeus,
pergolas, holiday beaches and sweet-smelling flowers. At the top is the aus-
tere mountain world of the Montenegrins, a harsh little state of being all
its own—different in landscape, different in climate, different in history,
different in kind.

As you round the last twist in that dizzy road, you find all about you
the bare and severe plateau of the Lovćen massif, like a plasticine landscape, corrugated here and there with what look like the runnels of ancient avalanches, waterless, apparently soil-less, and stubbled with arid
patches of scrub. You pass one bleak and windswept settlement, crouched

in a declivity in the plain, and there is nothing more, not a hut, not a barn, until in the middle of the wasteland suddenly you see before you, set in its own stony scoop among the hills, the city of Cetinje.

I call it a city for courtesy's sake, but it does not look like much from the road above: a long, tree-lined street—a cluster of buildings at the far end of it, a few splodges of green for parks or gardens, a scatter of houses around the edge. It looks like a not particularly welcoming oasis in a flinty highland desert. For more than 400 years, though, Cetinje was the capital of the Montenegrins, one of the most formidably independent peoples on the earth's surface; and more to our present point, for a decade or two around the turn of the century, it was also the undisputed capital of that indestructible kingdom of fantasy, Ruritania.

$$-o\,/\,o\,/\,o-$$

It has an air to it from the start. That long central avenue, which turns out to be called Boulevard Lenin, though bumpy from the winter snows and lined for the most part by undistinguished single-story houses, possesses a certain ceremonial feel. Cetinje (which is pronounced, more or less, *settinya*) is the capital of nowhere nowadays: the headquarters of the Socialist Republic of Crna Gora, one of the six constituent republics of Yugoslavia, has moved up the road to Titograd. But Cetinje has been for so long important in its own eyes, and intermittently in the eyes of others, that it is infused with an exhilarating sensation of swagger. Its people are very handsome, and bear themselves magnificently. Its upland climate is stimulating. Its buildings—well, its buildings get odder as we progress down the street, and they give to the little town a curiously hallucinatory effect, like a cross between Hollywood and Turgenev.

It was not always Ruritania—just the contrary. Almost alone in the entire Balkans, the territory of the Christian Montenegrins was never conquered by the Turks. When all around them had succumbed, when Turkish armies were at the gates of Vienna, far to the north, when Turkish fleets lay in the Gulf of Kotor, just down the mountain, the indomitable Montenegrins never surrendered, habitually decorating their capital with the skulls of slaughtered Muslims and inculcating their children, generation after generation, with a savage and relentless defiance.

More than that, if they succeeded in preserving their political independence, they succeeded, too, in maintaining their peculiar way of life. They were ruled by prince-bishops, fighting prelates who combined all authority—spiritual, secular, and strategic—in one mighty office. It was the greatest of these men, the nineteenth-century leader Petar Njegoš, who brought the Montenegrin spirit to a climax and gave Cetinje its original fulfillment.

There is his palace now, that low grey building at the foot of the hill, more like a huge stable than a princely residence, overlooked by an unpretentious towered monastery on the slope behind. The palace is called the Biljarda, because it contains a billiard table (quarter size) presented to Njegoš by the Czar of Russia and brought on muleback up the Ladder. Njegoš adored billiards. Six foot six, marvellously good-looking, a crack shot, a learned jurist, a gifted linguist, the greatest poet of Montenegrin literature, he was heroic in all his enthusiasms, and he haunts the city still: his portrait in almost every bar, his palace a museum, his epic poems still in print, his tomb where he decreed it, high above the city on the summit of Mount Lovćen, looking down from that terrific vantage point (in winter deep in snow) upon his devoted little capital.

But it is not Njegoš's Cetinje that we have come to see, and anyway it has long been overlaid by memories less tremendous. His was the tread of war, art, and learning. Now, as you leave your car outside the Biljarda and walk across the gravel into town, it is the beat of ghostly polkas that is more likely to reach you, bugle calls perhaps, shrill duets of comic opera, snatches of stagy dialogue. Njegoš died in the splendor of his middle years, leaving Cetinje a proud, cultured, and invincible capital; half a century later, his nephew's nephew Nicholas proclaimed himself king of Montenegro, and turned the place into a prodigy of another kind.

– o / o / o –

Only a stone's throw from the stern pile of the Biljarda, Nicholas's royal palace is something very different. From the outside it may not seem very imposing, and it reminds me indeed of a more than usually prosperous dry-goods store, with living quarters above the shop, in a midwestern country town. Inside, though, it is the very encapsulation of opéra bouffe—cockaded hats, chivalric orders, swords, white gloves and all.

Nicholas I, the first and last king of Montenegro, came to power in the heyday of the monarchical delusion, when emperors, kings, princes, and grand dukes lorded it all over Europe; and it was his delight, from his own modest and inaccessible seat of power, to picture himself among their egregious company. This fancy he assiduously translated into fact, and his palace is stuffed in every corner with Royalness. It is a museum of monarchy, a cabinet of kingship. On every wall hang portraits of crowned and coroneted heads—unimaginable empresses, unidentifiable princelings—that other Nicholas, the Czar of all the Russias—that other stickler for form the future George V of England, his portrait signed with a cramped hand and a forgivably misspelled Cetinje during his visit to Montenegro in 1887.

Your state-appointed guide takes you from crown to crown, court to court, with every sign of respect, reeling off the royal pedigrees as adeptly as any old retainer of the aristocratic past. Observe the wardrobe full of the king's stupendous uniforms. Note the dinner service presented by Napoleon III. Those stamps and coins, you will see, bear the head of His Majesty. That teak chair from Java was presented by the Czarina. Beneath the portrait of King Nicholas—This way! Step this way, please!—hangs a frock coat as worn by Montenegrin diplomatic representatives at foreign courts.

The fantasy thickens as you wander on; the dream proliferates. What staggering profusions of medals and orders, stacked with their gaudy ribbons in big glass cases, surmounted by the lions, the elephants, the peacocks, the bears and the miscellaneous chimeras of international chivalry! What elaborations of chinoiserie, rococo or Second Empire, presented to His Majesty by this potentate or that to celebrate one formal occasion or another! A gigantic polar-bear skin is spread on the kingly bedroom floor. A mournful tapestry depicting the composer Verdi—unaccountably presented to the palace, so the guide says, by George Bernard Shaw—hangs above the piano that Liszt is supposed to have played in one of the princesses' bedrooms.

For yes, the dynastically minded Nicholas fathered three little princes and nine princesses, and the trophies and emblems of their marital alliances, too, hang thick upon the walls of this remote Balkan villa, linking it astonishingly with the network of Schönbrunn, Windsor and Winter Palace. One daughter married the King of Italy, one the King of Serbia; two became the pair of grand duchesses who introduced Rasputin to the Russian court; and one gave birth, in a house just across the road from the palace, to the future King Alexander of Yugoslavia.

So King Nicholas really did realize his ambitions, and he furnished his house, top to bottom, with reminders of his lineage and achievement. He had made it: and everywhere, on badges and buttons, cutlery and cannon, the double-headed Eagle of Montenegro, elevated now to the status of a royal cipher, gave notice of his admission to the company of the Hapsburgs and the Romanovs.

−o / o / o−

All this panoply sits ironically in Cetinje. It is essentially a sinewy kind of town, not at all upholstered. There is nothing ample about it. It is built of a greyish monastic stone, and its buildings are low, giving it a crouching stance. All around the mountains grimly rise, and if the sky is often brilliantly blue, the landscape around the town is all monochrome. There is nothing much in the way of a main square, the most obvious focus of the place being a small church whose churchyard railings consist entirely, and characteristically, of the gun barrels of captured Turkish rifles. For the rest, Cetinje sprawls shapelessly around the southern end of Boulevard Lenin (which revealingly turns at its southern end into Njegoś Street). Its sidewalks are always full of lounging men and hurrying housewives. Its shops are communistically drab. Its policemen are Montenegrinally relaxed. Its style is easygoing but faintly arrogant.

Upon this mountain village, for it is hardly more even now, King Nicholas imposed the trappings of European consequence, and the powers of the day took him seriously. Encouraged by the astute if risible chieftain, they hastened to accredit their envoys to his ridiculous court, and their legations stand there still, converted into state institutions of one sort or another but still preposterously incongruous. For a few years they sustained, high on this uncomfortable plateau, all the pretense and protocol of *la vie diplomatique;* and there are a few aged plenipotentiaries still alive, retired long since from their careers, who remember being sent *en poste*—with sinking heart, I daresay, and ambitions temporarily flattened—to their country's mission in Cetinje.

The old Italian legation on the boulevard is the most elegant of them: it had to be, for the Princess Helen of Montenegro was Queen of Italy, and there were lofty comings and goings between Cetinje and Rome. It had an orangery, and it is surrounded by gardens of aromatic pines, pleasant for royal garden parties or diplomatic tête-à-têtes. On the other hand, the Imperial Russian legation is unquestionably the stateliest; it has fallen into decay now, after some years' service as a city hall, but is still evocative with flagpoles and sculptured symbolisms—you can almost see the dust rise still from the ministerial carriage wheels, and hear the hiss of the samovar in the ruined kitchens at the back.

The French legation was daringly built in an Art Deco style, the very latest thing then, and is stuck about with colored glass tiles and squiggly lamp brackets, and curiously angled. The British mission is like a country house, gentlemanly, discreet, and conveniently close to the palace of the Crown Prince. The Austrian legation has a private chapel, angel-embellished, as well as a sentry box at the gate. The Turks, who would seem lucky to have had a legation in Cetinje at all, sensibly made it as unobtrusive as possible, in case the Montenegrins decided they needed a few more decorative skulls. The Americans economically made do with rooms in the Grand Hotel, but this was not much sacrifice, for the Grand was the true center of Cetinje social life. It stands there still, near the foot of the town, though not at present open for business, and looks from its comfortable posture and spacious foyer as though it must have been just the place for a jolly diplomatic ball, or a party to celebrate somebody's National Day.

Imagine the life that hummed around these strange and anomalous structures in the days before the First World War—the presentations at the palace, with courtly aides and attentive major-domos, the invitations delivered by sashed messengers, the encounters of ministers' wives on Sunday promenades! The intrigues, too, no doubt—the confiding and betraying of diplomatic secrets, the catching of influential ears, the writing of tantalizing dispatches (for in those inflammatory days, when the Balkans were the tinderbox of Europe, Montenegro was all too often in the minds of statesmen).

King Nicholas adored it all, of course, and made sure that no nicety of modern monarchy was neglected. He commissioned a fine new building, designed by Italian architects and decorated with rampant griffins, to house his departments of state. He built a court chapel outside his garden wall. He devised becoming uniforms for his soldiers, who had hitherto won their victories without benefit of uniforms at all, and sometimes he reviewed them, attended by the entire diplomatic corps, from the first-floor balcony of his palace.

And across the road from the Russian legation he built that *sine qua non* of any capital city, an opera house. It is there still. It looks, it is true, a little like a town hall, and does not often stage an opera nowadays; but its little auditorium is infused with an unexpectedly innocent and poignant charm, an emanation of pleasures long ago enjoyed, of pretensions long ago discredited.

–o / o / o–

For all was swept away, levee to *Tosca,* by the scouring wind that was the Great War of 1914, leaving behind these quaint relics and reminders of the one and only king. And long before that, actually, the village grandeurs of the Cetinje court had suffered an apotheosis into frivolous parody. Anthony Hope, when he invented the kingdom of Ruritania for his *Prisoner of Zenda,* doubtless had the Montenegrin state in mind as the most improbable of all the petty Balkan monarchies. Franz Lehar certainly did when he wrote that resilient masterpiece of kitsch *The Merry Widow,* for its protagonist, the prince Danilo, is actually given a Montenegrin royal name. All the beloved absurdity of the musical-comedy court, which strutted the stages of the West for so many years, found its first and truest epitome here, far away among the fighting mountaineers of Lovćen.

It has its comic side still, the fantasy of Cetinje, but by now the old laughs have faded into suggestions melancholy and even tragic. Nicholas's prime model was the court of the Russian Romanovs. They were his closest allies, mentors, and exemplars. They accepted two of his daughters in royal alliance. They made him an honorary field marshal in the Imperial Army. They financed a lycée, next door to the Grand Hotel, where little Montenegrin girls could be trained into the lady-like disciplines of monarchy. The Montenegrin royal family was not murdered when their kingdom was abolished in 1918—they simply died off in exile—but it is still St. Petersburg that Cetinje, even now, hauntingly suggests. The little court chapel in its walled enclosure; the pine woods and the parks; the few old monks in their monastery up the hill; the very uniforms that hang in the king's closet, those ankle-hugging greatcoats, those stern-peaked caps—all are mementos, of a kind, of that other fated capital to the north. Spectral dance music welcomed us to Cetinje; imaginary fusillades salute our leaving.

No need to brave the Ladder again. Much easier roads lead down to the coast the southern way, to Budva. The images of that high plateau will pursue you nonetheless; not just the tinsel bravado of Nicholas's transient monarchy, nor even the grave eyes of the murdered Romanovs

on those bedroom walls, but things profounder still and more permanent—images of Montenegro itself, Njegoš's Montenegro, the Black
Mountain, which preceded these short-lived tomfooleries and survives
them still. It was only a moment of folly that we have been reliving in
the little town, and soon we are out of it all, back in the empty trenchant
wasteland, whose few houses are huddled still defiantly against wind,
time and earthquakes, and whose poet-prince looks down still (indulgently? ironically?) from his mausoleum on the mountaintop.

Capital of the Holy Faith

SANTA FE, U.S.A

The day starts late in Santa Fe, New Mexico. The sun is already high over mountain and mesa when the Indian traders emerge from their large if well-worn limousines in the central plaza beneath the portico of the Palace of the Governors—a museum now, but still claiming to be the Oldest Government Building in the United States. Silently they lay their rugs on the ground, open their collapsible chairs, set out for display their pots, bangles, earrings and blueberry jams, and settle down themselves, the more thoroughgoing of them picturesquely wrapped in blankets, to await the day's profit. They take little notice of each other. They slump down heavily and focus an expressionless gaze, a little glazed perhaps but awfully penetrating, unequivocally across the awakening plaza.

They have been around here for ever. Long before the gringos came in their wagons, long before the Spaniards with their cavalry, centuries even before the wandering Navajos or the raging Apache reached these parts, the Tewa and the Keres Indians lived in their adobe pueblos along the valley of the Rio Grande. The arrival of the white man has left them more or less cold to this day. Once, in 1680, they rose in rebellion against the Spaniards, but they were soon put down, and ever since they have lived in a condition of reasonably amiable but unforthcoming resignation, coming into town each day to plonk themselves down there beneath the venerable arcade. Nobody can move them now. Far from appearing an oppressed minority, in fancy at least they sometimes seem to hold the little city in their grip, ringing it with their inviolable pueblos, muddling it with ancient treaties, mystifying it with immemorial rites. There are only a few thousand of them in the neighborhood, but of all the 50,000 habitués of Santa Fe they seem much the most confident of their *genre*.

–o / o / o–

If you enter the museum and sit on one of its window seats, the glossy black head of one of those traders outside will be immediately beside you through the glass, and you may look at the rest of Santa Fe more or less through his eyes. How confusing a community it must seem to him, out of his ageless continuities! Santa Fe is old enough itself, having been founded by the Spaniard Pedro de Peralta as La Villa Real de Santa Fe, the Royal Capital of the Holy Faith, in 1610: besides the Oldest Government Building it boasts the Oldest Church in the United States, and the Oldest House too. But though the place possesses great historical and hereditary charm, it is charm of a somewhat shambled and diffuse kind. Nothing is very firmly rooted, by Indian standards. The city stands at the foot of the mountains, on the edge of the desert, vulnerable and unsure.

Take the central square out there, which is full of small trees, and has an obelisk in the middle, and a clock in the shape of an old-fashioned pocket watch on a pillar at one corner. It looks rooted enough, being built for the most part in the Santa Fe adobe style, all mud, protruding beams and balconies. Woolworth's, Geppetto's Restaurant, Kahn's Shoe Store, the sprawling La Fonda Hotel—all are built in this agreeable form, and give the business quarter a harmonious unity. It is nearly all sham, though. Santa Fe's adobe is mostly less than mud-deep, being merely a cosmetic veneer over wood and concrete. Everything may look comfortably picturesque from our window behind the Indian's head, but out of sight beyond the Oldest Church, away behind the Palace of the Governors, Santa Fe "The City Different" sprawls away in a wide mélange of the all too same—ever-extending suburbs of mock adobe, the Rancho de This or the Camino del That, ribbon growths of tacky housing, gimcrack shops and discount warehouses, sleazy dumping grounds of shacks and trailers petering out among the desert shrub.

And consider the people, sauntering into view now over our Tewa's shoulder as he reaches out to adjust his stock, perhaps, with a silver wand made of an old car aerial. Santa Fe likes to call itself a tri-cultural community—Indian, Hispanic, Anglo—but it is really nothing so simple. It is a place of cross-currents, acculturizations, adoptions, blends, Indianized

Hispanics, Anglicized Anglos, born-again Spaniards singing evangelical hymns, Polish-descended migrants from Cedar Rapids drinking sangria and eating tortillas, full-blooded Indian braves having their hair permed in unisex salons. You see that cop there, so Castilian of command, so Andalusian of sideburn? He speaks not a word of Spanish. You see that Indian woman passing by, the one with the glittering eyes and the turquoise rings? She is a nice Jewish lady from Illinois. Even the Indians themselves, are not so cohesive as they look, obscure animosities having divided their several villages since the dawn of time.

An ever-shifting haze of part-time residents and visiting performers further complicate the scene. Here are some of the people I bumped into, rubbed shoulders with, successfully evaded, was repeatedly told about or failed to have calls returned by, during my own brief residence in Santa Fe: John Ehrlichman, the Duke of Bedford, the man who once held the record for the longest airline ticket ever issued, Lady Bird Johnson's brother, Neil Simon, the producer of the Jack Benny Show, Roger Miller, George McGovern, the head of the Gray Panthers, two or three Buddhist monks, several Greatest Living Southwestern Artists, more than one genius designer of Indian pots, and dozens of the American Sikhs, bearded, turbanned and daggered, who run the city's largest security company.

Out there this motley population is coming and going now, as the morning warms up: and always among them too, slowly peregrinating past our window beneath the arcade pass the tourists, respectfully for the most part, since they are over-awed by the Oldest Government Building in the United States, and forced into neurotic self-consciousness, like most gringos these days, by the presence of the Indians. They look everywhere but in our Tewa's eye, and when they buy a pendant, a belt or a beaded table-mat, they seem to make the purchase not exactly of their own volition, but in half-mesmerized embarrassment. We cannot see, of course, the expression on our particular Indian's face: but you may be sure his gaze is unblinking.

–o / o / o–

"This certainly is a cute area," I heard one visitor say to another nevertheless one day, when they were well away from the arcade, and there is no denying that Santa Fe's first impression upon the visitor is a somewhat silly one. Santa Fe is the artiest, sculpturest, weaviest and potteryest town on earth, and is accordingly thick with trivial parasites. There are shops with trivial names, like Tidbits or Eclectibles. There are galleries with trivial pictures, infantile Pop Art or Corn Dance oils. There are trivial experts everywhere, spouting the names of undiscovered virtuosi, expounding the especial redolence, mass or graininess of Hopi vases. Since I first came to this town, twenty-five years ago, Santa Fe has acquired more than its fair share of such dilettante nonsense, and the more fashionable the place becomes, the deeper it is sucked into what the town traditionalists like to call the Aspen syndrome.

You know what they mean. You know the people who will not on any account admit that they are newcomers to a place—eleven years, I discover, is the median term of residence claimed by Santa Feans, but very often they used to come here when they were children, too, of course, or had a grandmother native to the place (half Pueblo Indian, they were led to believe), or, oh, they just can't remember *when* they came, it was all so long ago. You know the irrepressible ethnic dresser or regional decorist: in Hawaii it's muumuus, in Maine it's wheel-back chairs, in Santa Fe it's all flouncy layered frocks with marsupial pouches, multitudinous silver jewelries and Navajo wall rugs.

Santa Fe is infested with poseurs, old fools dressed up like Wild Bill Hickock or presiding over chichi eating-houses, young fools still living, with flutes, cut-off jeans and pigtails, the vanished world of the hippies and the love-people—*"Here's a little song I wrote 'bout six months ago:*

> *Life goes on, life goes on,*
> *Sometimes you cry, and so do I. . . ."*

At first blush it all makes one feel that the town itself is hardly more than a pretense, perpetually striking poses too in false architecture and display. This is a mistake, though. In some ways Santa Fe is shammer than it looks, but in some ways more genuine. Real artists *are* painting here, honest craftsmen *are* at work, some of those gallery people truly respect the creative gift and history is not entirely fictionalized for the tourist trade.

– o / o / o –

Just along the road from the Palace of the Governors stands Sena Plaza, a complex of old buildings around a shady garden. Nothing could be more absolutely Santa Fe. A fountain daintily spouts beneath the trees there, and a characteristic gallimaufry of concerns has its premises all around: Rare Things, the Señor Murphy Candy Shop, "Tug" Wilson's oil company, the Girl Scouts, Watson, Stillinger and Lunt, attorneys at law, the Ancient City Bookshop, which specializes in works about women, healing and adobe. It is a delightful spot, calm, secluded and—well, cute.

But I have met a lady who lived in this photogenic compound when the whole of it was still her family house—a hacienda in the truest Spanish kind, with its big courtyard in the middle, with its stables behind, with its long ballroom on the first floor and its family altar set up by the gate each year when the procession of La Conquistadora passed by outside. In Mrs. Sanchez's grandfather's day it was staffed by innumerable Indian servants, and even in her own girlhood the family migrated every summer, when the heat began, out of Sena Plaza to the family ranch in the nearby countryside—now spectacularly transformed, as it happens, into a foundry and showroom for sculptors in metal, its gallery bucking with bronze broncos, its orchards littered with incomprehensible aluminium artifacts.

So sudden has been the seizure of Santa Fe by contemporary American civilization, so close is its Hispanic past. In many respects this is a Spanish city still. The most powerful man in town, some people say, is the Catholic Archbishop of Santa Fe (who lives in Albuquerque actually) and I am told that scarcely a political move can be made without considering the sensibilities of the Catholic church, whether it be the introduction of universal free abortion (unthinkable) or the granting of liquor licenses (negotiable). Family loyalties are strong, in the old Spanish way: the Chavez clan, which claims descent from King Ferdinand of León and Castile, held a reunion while I was in Santa Fe, and hundreds of Chavezes turned up from all over New Mexico. Family secrets thrive, too: incest is allegedly much more common than rape, and in the mountain villages of the Sangre de Cristo range, immediately behind the city, the closed orders of the Penitentes, emerging at dawn from their windowless *moradas,* still process into the hills during Passion Week in penance for the sins of the world. The febrile and oblique feeling of Santa Fe springs mostly from this old heritage, and I dare say a *little* of the inefficiency (for a good many things don't work too well). It is really not so long, after all, since genuine Spanish grandees ran this town, since missionary friars offered Mass in their lovely churches of mud and carved wood, or harangued the bewildered animists of the pueblos.

But like so much else in Santa Fe, the Spanish culture—*"Nuestra Cultura,"* as they like to say—seems uncertain of itself these days. It has been pressed upon so relentlessly by all the influences and temptations of the American way. Often in the evenings the cultists called the Low Riders cruise through town. They are the public face, I suppose, of young Hispanica: and as they slowly drive about the streets in their weirdly low-slung limousines, wearing wide hats and dark glasses, radios booming, unsmiling, proud, *stately* one really might say, who knows what resentments or aspirations of their race they are trying to declare?

–o / o / o–

This was Kit Carson country, the end of the Santa Fe Trail from Carson City, and it was here that the mountain men, the drovers, the traders and the homesteaders of the Anglo-American north met, mixed and struggled with the hidalgos, the priests, the vaqueros and the primitives of the Indo-Spanish south. If there are 167 Chavezes in the telephone book, there are also 117 Smiths; and if Santa Fe is still Spanish in style and temper, it is largely gringo in hard cash. The money in Santa Fe's banks, I am told, is largely Eastern money, the best customers for Santa Fe's galleries and boutiques are Texans and Southern Californians, and most of those new houses springing up around the perimeters of town are destined to be occupied by Anglos of one category or another.

Here and there one stumbles upon survivals of the days when Santa Fe's English-speaking citizens were mostly simple hometown folk—Bell's clothing store in San Francisco Street, for example, which has been selling its straw hats, its wedding dresses and its sensible children's shoes since 1926, and which still breathes a true Main Street integrity. There is nothing very fancy, for that matter, to many of the newcomers from elsewhere in the States who have come here to find jobs, to retire, or set up modest businesses in the sun. In reputation, though, Anglo Santa Fe is something very different: a leisured, influential and gentlemanly colony of settlers, long embedded in the city, less reminiscent of Carson's Old West than of cultivated Chicago suburbs, the less flamboyant alcoves of Beverly Hills or clapboard settlements of New England far away.

Such a colony exists. Behind the foolishness of the curio dealers and the gallery managers, beyond the flash of the entrepreneurs, the developers and the assorted trendies now falling on Santa Fe as they fell not so long ago upon Key West or Martha's Vineyard—in the core of Santa Fe society there thrives a well-read and well-heeled English-speaking community that has perhaps no exact equivalent elsewhere. It is eighty years now since the first gringo artists and intellectuals settled here, and half a century since the editor of *The New Mexican* numbered among the town's special assets "a group of creative people, artists, writers, sculptors, musicians, architects." The settlement thrived, and grew, and prospers still, opulent without being extravagant, sometimes eccentric but seldom showy, gossipy and cosmopolitan.

It is an aristocratic kind of society, Anglo in blood but subtly Hispanicized in spirit, keenly salted with Jewishness, despising ostentation, preferring the Volvo to the Porsche, and most certainly to the Cadillac. Old ladies *look* like old ladies. Books are bought to be read. Television is most often switched, I would surmise, if switched at all, to *Masterpiece Theatre,* and the great events of the year are the performances at the Opera House beside the Taos Road. Good, true art has been fostered by this community in its day, music flourishes under its patronage, and inasmuch as Santa Fe is known across the world, attracting foreigners of many kinds to live and work here, ringing a bell at least in most people's minds, the city owes it to this civilized enclave.

But it is under siege, too. Santa Fe, so recently hardly more than a remote and rather secretive village, is chic these days. The smart, the modish, the merely rich move in. The haven is embattled. The old hands watch thoughtfully as Santa Fe, *dear* Santa Fe, slowly but inexorably changes its character—as the condominiums spring up over the foothills, as the Soak Hot-Tub Club offers its twelve hot-tub suites with individual stereo and mood lighting, as downtown land reaches $100,000 an acre— as the triviality of things, the cuteness, the sham and the opportunism, spreads like a tinsel stain across the town.

– o / o / o –

Still the Indians sit there, and in the evening they pack up the remains of their stock, fold their blankets and drive away into the resplendent and terrible countryside of Santa Fe. They are the spirits of the place, and they seem to leave behind them always, always drifting through the city, nuances of the landscape—fragrant suggestions of pine and wood smoke and mountain wind, frightening suggestions of war and savagery.

The land is always near in Santa Fe, blue and grey in the cool evenings, shadowed in the early mornings, the mesas vast to the east, the

Sangre de Cristos hushed and protective to the west. The splendor of this setting means that whatever happens to Santa Fe, reality can never be altogether overwhelmed by pretense, just as no resort beside the open sea can be altogether ridiculous. There is a village called Chimayo, north of the town, that sums up for me these marvellous compensations of the site. Indian by origin, Spanish by ancient settlement, it is famous for a ranch-house restaurant, for a family of weavers and for Low Riders, but most especially for its Santuario, to which for many generations pilgrims of all races have made their way to seek solace or refreshment. A hole in the ground within this little church contains soil of miraculous powers, and so the faithful in their thousands go there to dust themselves in it, and often to leave their discarded sticks and crutches in gratitude.

I was drawn repeatedly to this holy place, which, apart from its other arcane virtues, has wonderfully defied the corrosions of tourism: and once I found there, all alone within the shrine, a family bathing themselves in that soil almost as if it were liquid—splashing it on their faces, rubbing it on their shins, washing their hands in it—the father gravely reverent, the mother shy but happy, the little boy on his knees enthusiastically disregarding the injunction on the wall that says PLEASE DO NOT THROW HOLY DIRT OUTSIDE HOLE.

They smiled at me with a kind of confidential ecstasy; as if to imply that we at least, the lucky four of us, whatever went on in that criss-cross town below, knew where to scoop the simple truth.

Very Strange Feeling

A CHINESE JOURNEY

And in the distance, through the porthole, there stood China.

Of course wherever you are in the world, China stands *figuratively* there, a dim tremendous presence somewhere across the horizon, sending out its coded messages, exerting its ancient magnetism over the continents. I had been prowling and loitering around it for years, often touched on the shoulder by its long, long reach—watching the Chinese-Americans shadow-box in San Francisco, say, or being dragged screaming and kicking to the Chinese opera somewhere, or interviewing renegade patriots in Taiwan, or debating whether to go to the fish-and-chip shop or the Cantonese take-away in Dublin. It had seemed to me always the land of the grand simplicities, pursuing its own mighty way through history, impassive, impervious, where everything was more absolute than it was elsewhere, and the human condition majestically overrode all obstacles and reversions. I had wondered and marvelled at it for half a lifetime: and here I was at last on my way to meet it face to face, on a less than spanking Chinese steamship, rust-streaked, off-white, red flag at the stern, steaming steadily northward through the blue-green China Sea.

My fellow-passengers assiduously prepared me for the encounter. They showed me how best to suck the goodness out of the smoked black carp at dinner. They taught me to count up to ten in Mandarin. They drew my attention to an article in *China Pictorial* about the propagation of stink-bugs in Gandong Province. Mrs. Wang, returning from a visit to

her sister in Taiwan, vividly evoked for me her hysterectomy by acu-
puncture ("when they slit me open, oh, it hurt very bad, but after it was
very *strange* feeling, very *strange* . . ."). The Bureaucrat, returning from
an official mission to Hong Kong, thoroughly explained to me the Four
Principles of Chinese Government policy.

Around us the sea was like a Chinese geography lesson, too. It was
never empty. Sometimes apparently abandoned sampans wallowed in the
swell, sometimes flotillas of trawlers threshed about the place. Red-flagged
buoys mysteriously bobbed, miles from anywhere, grey tankers loomed
by high in the water. Islands appeared, islands like pimples in the sea,
like long knobbly snakes, islands with lighthouses on them, or radio
masts, or white villas. And always to the west stood the hills of China,
rolling sometimes, sheer sometimes, and once or twice molded into the
conical dome-shapes that I had hitherto supposed to be the invention of
Chinese calligraphers. Ah, but I must go far inland, the Bureaucrat told
me on our third day at sea, I must go to Guangxi in the south, to see
such mountains properly—mountains like no others, said he, the Peak of
Solitary Beauty, the Hill of the Scholar's Servant—"But look" (he interrupted himself)—"you notice?—the water is turning yellow. We are
approaching the mouth of the Yangtze!"

So we were. In the small hours that night, when I looked out of my
porthole again, I found we were sailing through an endless parade of
ships, gloomily illuminated in the darkness: and when at crack of dawn
I went on deck to a drizzly morning, still we were passing them, up a
scummy river now, lined with ships, thick with ships, barges, and tugs,
and container ships, and a warship or two, and country craft of shambled
wood so fibrous and stringy-looking that it seemed to me the Chinese,
who eat anything, might well make a dish of them. Hooting all the way
we edged a passage up the Huangpu, narrowly avoiding ferry-boats,
sending sampans scurrying for safety, until after thirty miles of ships,
and docks, and grimy warehouses, and factories, we saw before us a
waterfront façade of high towers and office buildings, red and shabby in
the rain. It was my China landfall: it was the city of Shanghai.

−o / o / o−

"Moonlight Serenade!" demanded the elderly American tourists in the
bar of the Peace Hotel, "Play it again!" The band obliged—half a dozen
well-worn Chinese musicians, a lady at the piano, an aged violinist, an

excellent trumpeter: Glenn Miller lived again in Shanghai, and the old thump and blare rose to a deafening climax and a smashing roll of drums. The Americans tapped their feet and shook their hands about, exclaiming things like "Swing it!." The band's eyes, I noticed, wandered here and there, as though they had played the piece once too often.

They have been playing it, after all, since they and the song were young. Their musical memories, like their personal experiences, reached back through Cultural Revolution, and Great Leap Forward, and People's Revolution, and Kuomingtang, and Japanese Co-Prosperity Zone, back through all the permutations of Chinese affairs to the days of cosmopolitan Shanghai—those terrible but glamorous times when European merchants lived like princes here, Chinese gangsters fought and thrived, the poor died in their hundreds on the sidewalks, and the Great World House of Pleasure offered not only singsong girls and gambling tables, but magicians, fireworks, strip shows, story-tellers, mah-jong schools, marriage brokers, freak shows, massage parlors, porn photographers, a dozen dance platforms and a bureau for the writing of love-letters.

No wonder the musicians looked world-weary. The Great World is the Shanghai Youth Palace now, the past of its former prostitutes being known only, we are primly told, to their Revolutionary Committee leaders. The band plays on all the same, and in many other ways too I was taken aback to find Old Shanghai surviving despite it all. The Race Club building, it is true, has been transformed into the Shanghai Public Library, and the racetrack itself is partly the People's Square, and partly the People's Park, but nearly everything else still stands. The pompous headquarters of the merchant houses still line the Bund, along the waterfront, surveying the tumultuous commerce that once made them rich. The Customs House still rings out the hours with a Westminster chime. The celebrated Long Bar of the Shanghai Club, which used to serve the best martinis at the longest bar in Asia, is propped up now by eaters of noodles with lemonade at the Dongfeng Hotel. The Peace Hotel itself is only the transmogrified Cathay, where Noel Coward wrote *Private Lives,* with its old red carpets still in place, 135 different drinks still on its bar list, and the Big Band sound ringing nightly through the foyer.

Even the streets of Shanghai, where the poor die no longer, seemed unexpectedly like home. There are virtually no private cars in this city of 11 million people, but I scarcely noticed their absence, so vigorously jostled and tooted the taxis, the articulated buses and the myriad bicycles: if there were few bright flowered clothes to be seen along the boulevards, only open-neck shirts and workaday slacks, there were still fewer of the baggy trousers, blue jerkins and Mao caps that I had foreseen. The theme music from *Bonanza* sounded through Department Store No. 10; there were cream cakes at Xilailin, formerly Riesling's Tea Rooms; the Xinya Restaurant still ushered its foreigners, as it had for a hundred years, into the discreet curtained cubicles of its second floor. On my first morning in Shanghai I ate an ice-cream in the People's Park (admission 2 *feng*), and what with its shady trees and winding paths, the old men playing checkers at its concrete tables, the students at their books, the health buffs at their calisthenics, the miscellaneous meditators and the tall buildings looking through its leaves above, I thought it, but for an absence of muggers and barouches, remarkably like Central Park.

Mrs. Wang had invited me to lunch at her apartment, and this was no culture shock, either. True, we ate eggs-in-aspic, a kind of pickled small turnip, and strips of a glutinous substance which suggested to me jellified sea-water, but nevertheless hers was a home that would not seem unduly exotic in, say, Cleveland. It was the bourgeois home *par excellence*. It had the statutory upright piano, with music open on the stand, the 16-inch color TV on the sideboard, a picture of two kittens playing with a ball of wool, a bookshelf of paperbacks and a daily help. It had a daughter who had come over to help cook lunch, and a husband away at the office who sent his regards. "We are very lucky," said kind Mrs. Wang. "We have a certain social status."

— o / o / o —

So this was *China?* I had to pinch myself. The Dictatorship of the People (Principle of Government number three, I remembered) does not visibly discipline Shanghai. Occasionally bespectacled soldiers of the People's Revolutionary Army trundle through town on rattly motor-bikes with sidecars, and outside the Municipal Headquarters (*né* Hong Kong and Shanghai Bank) two fairly weedy-looking troopers stand on sheepish sentry-go. Otherwise Authority is inconspicuous. The traffic flows in cheerful dishevellment over the intersections, ineffectually chivvied along over loudspeakers by policemen smoking cigarettes in their little white kiosks. Jay-walkers proliferate, and in the crinkled back-streets of the old quarter there seems no ideological restraint upon the free-enterprise pedlars and stall-holders, with their buckets of peaches, their plastic bags of orange juice, eels squirming in their own froth and compounds of doomed ducks.

Nobody seemed shy of me. Everyone wanted to talk. A factory worker I met in the park took me off without a second thought to his nearby apartment (two dark rooms almost entirely occupied by cooking utensils and bicycles), and the only hazard of the Shanghai street, I discovered, was the student who wished to practice his English. Stand just for a moment on the Bund, watching the ships go by, or counting the flitting sea-bats in the evening, and you are hemmed in, pressed against the balustrade, squeezed out of breath, by young men wanting to know if the word "intend" can legitimately be followed by a gerund. Go and lick an ice-cream in the park, and like magic there will materialize out of the trees Mr. Lu and a troop of elderly friends, all of whom remember with affection their English lessons with Miss Metcalfe at the Mission School, but none of whom has ever been *quite* sure about the propriety of the split infinitive.

Well! So this was the policy of the Open Door, which is bringing modernity to China, and has made foreigners and all their ways respectable. It seemed remarkably liberating. I often talked politics with people I met, and their answers sounded uninhibited enough. The Cultural Revolution, that hideous upheaval of the 1960s? A terrible mistake, a tragedy. The future of China? Nobody knew for sure what kind of country this was going to be. Communism versus Capitalism? There was good and bad in both. Would they like to go to America? Of course, but they would probably come home again. What a kind face Chou en-Lai had! Yes, he had a lovely face, he was a good kind man, the father of his people. Did they like the face of Mao Zedong?

Ah, but there was a hush when I asked this question. They thought for a moment. Then—"We don't know," was the mumbled answer, and suddenly I realized that they had not been frank with me at all. Not a reply had they given, but was sanctioned by the political orthodoxy of the moment. Did they like the *face* of Chairman Mao? He was a great man they knew, he had fallen into error in his later years, it had been admitted, but nobody it seems had ever told them whether to like his *face*. My perceptions shifted there and then, and where I had fancied frankness, now I began to sense evasions, veils or obliquities everywhere. This was, I reminded myself, the very birthplace and hot-bed of the Gang of Four, that clique of xenophobic zealots—it was from an agreeable half-timbered villa near the Zoo, Frenchified in a bowered garden, that their murderous frenzies were first let loose. A decade ago I might have had a very different greeting in Shanghai, and Mrs. W. would probably have been banished to one of the remoter onion-growing communes for giving me lunch.

No, perhaps it was not so home-like, after all. On the Bund one evening a man with the droopy shadow of a moustache pushed his way through the crowd and confronted me with a kind of dossier. Would I go through this examination paper for him, and correct his mistakes? But I had done my grammatical duty, I considered, for that afternoon, and I wanted to go and look at the silks in Department Store No. 10. "No," said I. "I won't."

At that a theatrical scowl crossed the student's face, screwing up his eyes and turning down the corners of his mouth. He looked, with that suggestion of whiskers round his chin, like a Chinese villain in a bad old movie, with a gong to clash him in. I circumvented him nevertheless, and ah yes, I thought in my newfound understanding, if the Gang of Four were still around you would have me up against a wall by now, with a placard around my neck, and a mob there to jeer me, not to consult me about participles!

–o / o / o –

As it was, I hasten to add, every single soul in Shanghai was kind to me, and as a matter of fact my conscience pricked me, and I went back and corrected his damned papers after all. The Open Door really is open in this city, and Foreign Guests are enthusiastically welcomed, from package tourists shepherded by guides in and out of Friendship Stores to bearded language students scooting about on bicycles. Back-packers labor through town in search of dormitories: peripatetic writers hang over the girders of Waibaidu Bridge watching the barges pass below.

Of these categories, the peripatetic writer seems the hardest for the Chinese mind to accommodate. "What is your *field?*" Mr. Lu asked me. I answered him with a quotation from the Psalms, to the effect that my business was simply to grin like a dog and run about the city. "You are a veterinary writer?" he inquired. Other people urged me to contact the Writers' Association, or at least to visit the new quarters on the northeast of the city, "where many intellectuals live," so that we could discuss common literary problems. Just running about the city did not satisfy them. It could not be productive.

One night I went to the acrobats, as every Shanghai visitor must, and realized with a jerk—I choose the word deliberately—what the sense of role means in China. There have been professional acrobats in this country for more than 2000 years, and in Shanghai they have an air-conditioned circular theatre, elaborately equipped with trapdoors, pulleys and chromium trapezes, for their daily performances of the all-but-incredible. They were astonishing, of course. They leapt and bounced around like chunks of rubber, they hurled plates across the stage faster than the eye could see, they balanced vast pyramids of crockery on tops of poles while standing on one foot on each other's heads, they were yanked to appalling standstills after falling headlong out of the roof.

"It is interesting to think," said my companion, "that in the Old China acrobats were like gypsies, of very low status. Now they are honored performers. They have their role in society." They were slotted, in short, and as I watched them it seemed to me that they not only had acrobats' limbs, and muscles, and eyes, but acrobats' thoughts, too, acrobats' emotions, specifically acrobatic libidos, and I fancied that if you stripped away their masks of acrobat make-up, there would only be other masks below, left behind from previous performances.

And it dawned on me that all those homely shuffling Shanghai crowds could be slotted too, if you had the key, into their inescapable roles. They were not really, as I had thought at first, at all like crowds of Third Avenue or Oxford Street. Every single citizen out there had his allotted place in the order of things, immutable: not a layabout loitered on those sidewalks, not an actor resting, not a busker, hardly a worker out of a job. What is your field? I am a Housewife. I am a Retired Worker. I am a Peasant. I am an Acrobat. I am a Student, and would be much obliged, please, if you would explain to me in simple language the meaning of the following English sentence. . . .

I did see one beggar in Shanghai, on the pavement opposite the former Park Hotel (famous once for its Sky Terrace, whose roof rolled back above the dance floor). He seemed to have broken his leg, and sat all bowed and bandaged, sobbing, while an associate held up an X-ray of the fracture. I am a Beggar, it seemed to say! The passers-by looked horrified, but whether by the mendicant himself, or by the nature of his injuries, I was unable to determine, the Shanghai dialect not being my field.

−o / o / o−

I went to the Yu Garden from a sense of duty—it is a National Protected Treasure, even though it was built in pure self-indulgence by an official of the Ming Dynasty, who caused its Rockery Hill to be constructed out of boulders brought from thousands of miles away and stuck together with rice-glue. I was ensnared there, however, by the children. There must have been a hundred of them outside the Hall for the Viewing of Rockery Hill, all three or four years old, some of them tied together with string to prevent them straying off into the Hall for Watching Swimming Fish, and I wasted a good half-hour playing with them. What adorable merry faces! What speed of mood and response, mock-terror, sham-apprehension, sheer hilarity! I stayed with them until they were led off two by two, a long crocodile of black-haired roly-poly imps, towards the Hall of Jade Magnificence.

There is nowhere like Shanghai for infant-watching, but in the end, among all the increasingly puzzling and deceptive inhabitants of this city, it was the children who baffled me most. They have a particular fondness for foreigners, and will pick one out from miles away, across a crowded square, clean through the Tower of Lasting Clearness, to wiggle an introductory finger. They have no apparent vices. They never cry, they don't know how to suck a thumb, and though their trousers are conveniently supplied with open slits in their seats, I am sure they never dirty themselves anyway.

How I wished I could get inside their little heads, and experience the sensations of a People's Revolutionary childhood! Do they never fret, these infants of the Middle Kingdom? Is that sweet equanimity of theirs force-fed or innate, ethnic or indoctrinated? Could it really be that this society is bringing into being a race that needs no diapers? The children in the Yu Garden waved and made funny faces at me as they stumped away, but they left me uneasy all the same.

So next day I went to one of the notorious Children's Palaces, after-school centers where children can either have fun, or be coached in particular aptitudes. I say notorious, because for years these places have been shown off to visiting foreigners, so that they long ago acquired the taint of propaganda. Certainly through my particular Palace a constant succession of tourist groups was passing, led by the hand by selected infants in somewhat sickly intimacy, and in the course of the afternoon the children presented a musical show, mostly of the Folk-Dance-from-Shanxi-Province kind, which did seem short on innocent spontaneity, and long on ingratiation.

But what disturbed me more than the stage management was the utter oblivion of the children themselves to the peering, staring, bulb-flashing tourists led all among them, room by room, by those minuscule trusties (who have an unnerving habit, by the way, of calling their charges *Auntie*). With an uncanny disregard they continued their ping-pong or their video games, pedalled their stationary bicycles, made their model ships, practised their flutes, repeated once again that last crescendo in the Harvest-Song-of-the-Yugur-Minority, or sat glued to the pages of strip-cartoon books, turning their pages with what seemed to me an unnatural rapidity. Their eyes never once flickered in our direction. Their attention never wavered. They simply pursued their activities with an inexorable concentration, never idle, never squabbling, just turning those pages, batting those balls, pedalling those pedals, twanging those strings or piping those Chinese flutes.

I was bemused by them. Were they really reading at all? Were they even playing, in our sense of the verb? Search me! I can only report one odd little episode, which sent me away from the Children's Palace peculiarly uncomfortable, and came to color my whole memory of Shanghai. Early in a performance of "Jingle Bells" by an orchestra of children under the age of five, the virtuoso lead xylophonist happened to get herself a full tone out of key. She never appeared to notice; nor did any of the other performers, all dimples, winsome smiles and bobbing heads up there on the stage. On they went in fearful discord, tinkle-tinkle, clang-clang, simpering smugly to the end.

– o / o / o –

The airline magazine on CAAC Flight 1502, Shanghai to Beijing, was six months old (and reported the self-criticism of a Chinese women's vol-ley-ball team defeated by Americans in 1982—"they were desperate with fiery eyes, whereas we were passive and vulnerable to attack"). It was like flying in a dentist's waiting-room, I thought. Also the seats in the 707 seemed to be a job lot from older, dismembered aircraft, some of them reclining, some of them rigid, while people smoked unrestrictedly in the non-smoking section, and our in-flight refreshment was a mug of luke-warm coffee brought by a less than winning stewardess. I was not surprised by all this. I was lucky, I knew, that there were no wicker chairs in the middle of the aisle, to take care of over-booking, and at least we were not called upon, as passengers on other flights have been, to advance *en masse* upon reactionary hijackers, bombarding them with lemonade bottles.

The enigmas were mounting. Why, I wondered, were the Chinese modernizing themselves with such remarkable ineptitude? Did they not invent the wheelbarrow a thousand years before the West? Had they not, for that matter, split the atom and sent rockets into space? Were they not brilliantly quick on the uptake, acute of observation, subtle of inference? The broad-minded Deng Xiaoping is boss man of China these days, and he is dedicated to technical progress of any derivation—as he once said in a famous phrase, what does it matter whether a cat is black or white, so long as it catches mice? China simmers all over with innovation and technology from the West: yet still the coffee's cold on Flight 1502.

The brick-laying of contemporary China would shame a backyard amateur in Arkansas. The architecture is ghastly. In the newest and grandest buildings cement is cracked, taps don't work, escalators are out of order. *Respect Hygiene,* proclaim the street posters, but the public lavatories are vile, and they have to put spittoons in the tombs of the Ming Emperors. Western architects, I am told, often despair to find air-conditioning connected to heating ducts, or fire-escapes mounted upside-down, and though it is true that the Chinese-made elevators in my Shanghai hotel were the *politest* I have ever used, with buttons marked Please Open and Please Close, still I felt that all the courtesy in the world would not much avail us if we ever got stuck halfway.

Why? What happened to the skills and sensibilities that built the Great Wall, molded the exquisite dragon-eaves, dug out the lovely lakes of *chinoiserie?* Feudalism stifled them, the official spokesmen say. Isolation atrophied them, the historians maintain. Maoism suppressed them, say the pragmatists. Communism killed them, that's what, say the tourists knowingly. But perhaps it goes deeper than that: perhaps the Chinese, deprived of their ancient magics, observing that nothing lasts, come Ming come Mao, have no faith in mere materialism, and put no trust in efficiency. *Feng shui,* the ancient Chinese geomancy which envisaged a mystic meaning to the form of everything, is banned from the People's Republic; and dear God, it shows, it shows.

Never mind: with an incomprehensible splutter over the public address system, and a bit of a struggle among those who could not get their tables to click back into their sockets, we landed safely enough in Beijing.

-o/o/o-

The first thing that struck me about this prodigious capital, which commands the destinies of a quarter of the earth's inhabitants, was the nature of its light. It was a continental light, a light of steppes or prairies, and it seemed to be tinged with green. At first I thought of it as metallic, but later it seemed to me more like concrete: arched in a vast bowl over the capital, a sky of greenish concrete!

And concrete too was the dominant substance of the city down below: stacks of concrete, yards of concrete, parks paved with concrete, their trees ignominiously sunk in sockets of soil, vast highways like concrete glaciers across the city, and everywhere around the flat skyline the looming shapes of high-rise blocks, their grim squareness broken only by the outlines of cranes lifting final concrete slabs to their summits. No need for rice-glue, I concluded, in Beijing.

I was staying on the outskirts of the city, almost in the country. There the concrete was interrupted often by fields of vegetables, and the traffic that passed in the morning was half-rural—mule-carts all among the buses, juddering tractors sometimes. Most of the drivers looked half-dead with fatigue, so early had they awoken in the communes, I suppose, and the traffic itself seemed to rumble by in monotonous exhaustion. I went one morning to the Lugou Bridge, which used to be the city limit for foreigners, and standing there amongst its 282 sculpted lions, all different, above its green-rushed river, watched those tired reinforcements laboring into the city: on the next bridge upstream, big black puffing freight trains, wailing their whistles and snorting; on the next bridge to the south, bumper to bumper an unbroken line of ugly brown trailer-trucks; across the old structure beside me, past the ancient stele eulogizing Morning Moonlight on Lugou Bridge, half a million bicyclists, half-awake, half-asleep, lifeless on their way to work.

Somewhere over there, I knew, was the source and fulcrum of the Chinese presence—the Inner City of Beijing, which used to be Peking, which used to be Peiping, which was Kubla Khan's Dadu—the home of Deng Xiaoping, the home of Chairman Mao, the home of the Manchu Emperors, and the Mings and the Hans before them. I approached it warily.

Like the supplicants of old China, kept waiting for a year or two before granted audience with the Son of Heaven, I hung around the fringes of the place, waiting for a summons.

I grinned a lot, and ran (but not too energetically, for the temperature was around 95° Fahrenheit). If Shanghai felt at first unexpectedly familiar, Beijing seemed almost unimaginably abroad. Everything was different here. The faces were different, the eyes were different, the manners were colder and more aloof. Nobody wanted help with gerunds. Though as it happened people were more attractively dressed than they had been in Shanghai, far more girls in skirts and blouses, even a few young men in suits and ties, still they were infinitely more alien to me. The children, their heads often shaved or close-clipped, their cheek-bones high, did not respond so blithely. A sort of grave and massive contemplation greeted me wherever I went, as though through each pair of thoughtful eyes all the billion Chinese people, Jilin to Yunnan, were inspecting me as I passed.

Beneath that great green sky, treading those interminable concrete pavements, I felt awfully far from home: and when I followed the immemorial tourist route, and took a car to the Great Wall at Badaling, there on the sun-blazed masonry, looking out across those vast northern plains and purpled mountains, I felt I was breaking some strange and lifelong dream. The Wall has been reconstructed around Badaling Gate, and is over-run there by tourists of all nationalities, milling among the cars and buses below, having their pictures taken, riding the resident camel, eating little peaches and drinking Kekou Kele, "Tasty and Happy"—Coke, that is. It is easy to escape them, though. You make the fearfully steep ascent away from the gate towards the watchtower to the west ("We certainly are thankful to you, Mr. Kung," I heard a sweating American businessman unconvincingly gasp, as he dragged himself, temples pulsing, up these formidable steps, "for making this trip possible— isn't this a *great* trip, you guys?").

Once at the tower, you find that beyond it the wall is reconstructed no further, but degenerates instantly into crumbled stone and brickwork, rambling away over the undulating ridges with nobody there at all. I walked a long way along it, out into the empty countryside, all silent but for the wind, all lifeless but for the hairy caterpillars which crossed and re-crossed the uneven stonework beneath my feet. But lo, when in the middle of nowhere I sat down upon the parapet to think about my rather lonely situation, out of that wilderness four or five wispy figures emerged, and opening paper bags and wrappings of sackcloth, asked if I wished to buy some antique bells or back-scratchers. Yet again, China had topsy-turvied me. I had fallen among old acquaintances, and when one by one they took turns to look through my binoculars, well, said I to myself, what's so strange about the Great Wall of China, anyway?

Looked at from the east, Beijing is not remote at all—only 100 miles from the sea, only three hours or so by air from Tokyo. It is only when you come to it out of the west, or more pertinently out of the Western sensibility, that it remains so romantically distant. On a Monday after-noon I went down to the gigantic railway station, twin-towered and green-roofed (escalator out of order) to see the arrival of the Trans-Siberian Express from Moscow. This was a dramatic occasion. Hundreds of us had come to meet the train, for hours beforehand we waited in the cavernous International Travellers' Waiting Room, and when the bell rang, the great doors were opened and we burst on to the platform, an air of headiest expectancy prevailed. We stood on one leg, so to speak, we stood on the other—we looked at our watches again, we sat down, we got up—we gave the children another bottle of Kekou Kele to keep them quiet—and there, slowly round the curve into the station, very, very grandly appeared the Trans-Siberian.

With a triumphant blast of its whistle it came majestically to Beijing, the three engineers in their cab sitting there like a trio of admirals on a flagship bridge, and the waiting people clapped, and cheered, and waved newspapers, as the doors opened and from Mongolia or Siberia, Omsk or Moscow itself, their travel-worn loved ones fell home into China. One coach was full of a Western travel group: and these voyagers, as they emerged glazed and haggard on the platform, looking wonderingly around them, reminded me of the long-lost pilots returning to earth out of the space ship, in the closing sequences of *Close Encounters*.

– o / o / o –

There is not much left of Old Peking, except for Protected Treasures. The city walls have been torn down, most of the fortress gates have van-ished, the clutter of medievalism which so entranced the old travellers has been swept away as though it never were. Across the face of the central city has been laid the cruel thoroughfare called Changan, down which the trolley-buses trundle and the bikes chaotically swarm. Here and there though, all the same, I felt a powerful tug of organic continuity, in this city of 2000 years.

I felt it for instance at the Summer Palace of the last of the Manchu Empresses, which is now a public park, but is still everyone's idea of a Chinese imperial retreat, with its pagodas and its towering temples, its ornamental bridges among the water-lilies, its myriad boats upon the limpid lake, its covered way, decorated with a thousand scenes of Chinese legend, from which it is said no pair of lovers can emerge unbetrothed, and its ridiculous Marble Paddle-Steamer for ever moored beside the quay (the Empress built the place with money intended for the reconstruction of the Chinese navy, and commissioned this nautical folly, they say, as a slap in the face of the outraged Fleet).

I sensed the constancy of things ominously when, lifting my head unawares as I walked up Qianmen Street, I saw the vast glowering shape of the Qianmen Gate blocking the thoroughfare in front, for all the world as though it were still the portentous gateway, as it used to be, into the Inner City beyond. I sensed it delectably beside the lonely neglected pagoda of Balizhuang, twittered about by martins out on the western outskirts, at whose feet the women of the local commune worked crouching in their straw hats among the beanpoles, chitter-chattering half-hidden like so many swallows themselves. I felt it pungently in the traditional pharmacy called The Shared Benevolence Hall, founded in 1669, which is a treasure-house of arcane specifics, stack upon stack of mysterious powders, brown bottles of roots and seeds, phials of restorative nuts, seahorses, antlers, extract of deer-tail, heart of monkey. . . .

In the early mornings I used to go wandering through the *hutongs,* the crooked quarters of small courtyard houses which survive here and there off the huge new highways. A curious hush pervades these parts. No motor-traffic goes along the alley-ways, high walls conceal the jumbled yards. Only by peering through half-open gates can you glimpse the tangled, crowded life within, meshed in laundry and potted plants, here a man in no shirt eating porridge from a tin bowl, there an old woman smoking her first cigarette of the day, or a girl in a spotless white blouse extracting her bicycle from the rubble. A faint haze of smoke hangs in the air, and from the public lavatory, smelling violently of mingled excrement and disinfectant, heavy breathing and a vigorous swishing of brooms show that some unprivileged comrade is fulfilling early-morning labor norms.

Nobody ever took much notice of me, wandering these quiet lanes as the sun came up: only a fairly hooded eye focussed on me now and then, when a woman emerged to empty her slops down a drain, or a bicycle bell chivvied me out of the way.

And once very early I strayed over a bridge to a leafy path beside a moat. I was led there by a curious cacophony of shouts, singing and twanged instruments, and I found it to be the most hauntingly timeless place of all. It was a place of self-fulfillment. Resolutely facing a high stone rampart above the moat, like Jews at the Wailing Wall, all along the path men and women were rehearsing their own particular accomplishments privately in the dawn. As we sing in the evening tub, so the people of Beijing go to that wall. Here was a man, his face a few inches from the masonry, declaiming some heroic soliloquy. Here a woman was practising an astonishing range of arpeggios, shrill soprano to resonant baritone. A splendid bass was singing a romantic ballad, a poet seemed to be trying out a lyric, an old man with a bicycle was plucking the strings of an antique lute. I thought of joining in, so universal did these impulses seem, sending To Be or Not To Be reverberating down that wall, or perhaps reciting some of my own purpler passages: but I restrained myself, as a Foreign Guest, and just whistled my way home to breakfast.

–o / o / o–

I must have walked a hundred miles! and gropingly I circled towards the center of things—to what the old Chinese would have called the center of *all* things. The measured and muffled restraint of this city was like a fog in the sunshine. Gentle, un-pushing, polite, its people kept me always wondering, and I missed the flash of under-life that gives most great cities their clarity. I missed scamps, drunks, whores, hagglers, ticket touts offering me seats (which Heaven forfend) for the Chinese opera. I saw no Dostoievsky brooding over his minced shrimps, no tragic rebel sticking up wall posters. All seemed in bland order. I had been told to look out, in the dizzily Westernized new Jianguo Hotel, for Party officials in expensive suits taking luncheon with their mistresses: but all I saw were security guards from the American Embassy, eating Weight-Watchers' Salad.

How bored this quarter of the earth must be! Even the procreation of

the urban Chinese is limited, if not by law, at least by powerful persua-
sion. They must not gamble, there is nowhere to dance, it is miles on a
bike to a cinema, and if they turn the TV on, what do they get but im-
proving documentaries, English lessons, historical dramas of suitable im-
port or Chinese opera. Their one emotional release seems to be eating,
which they do with a gusto in which all their passions are surely subli-
mated. The grander restaurants of Beijing generally have two sections,
one for bigwigs and foreigners, the other for the masses: but though the
downstairs rooms are usually rough and ready, with linoleum tablecloths
and creaky old electric fans, an equal riotous festivity attends them all.

No wonder the Chinese are such hypochondriacs. They live so strangely,
I was coming to feel, in a condition of such crossed uncertainty and brain-
wash, that psychotic illness must be rampant. I went to one restaurant devoted to the cult of Dinetotherapy, sponsored by another 300-year-old
herb store, and was not surprised to find it prospering mightily. When I
told the waiter I was suffering from headaches and general debility, he
prescribed Sautéed Chicken with Fruit of Chinese Wolfberry, followed
by Giant Prawns Steamed in Ginger. They worked a treat: I walked out
feeling terrific.

But not all the prawns in China can cure the stresses of history, and the
real malaise of Beijing, I came to think, was its domination by an ideology so all-pervading, so arbitrary, in many ways so honorable, but apparently so inconstant, which can change the very way the nation thinks
from one year to another. Today it is liberal and welcoming, Chinese tradition is honored, people are free to wear what they like, consort with
foreigners if they will, sell their ducks in a free market and even build
themselves houses with the profits. Yesterday it was puritanically narrow,
the revolutionary condition was permanent, aliens were devils, Mao caps
and floppy trousers were *de rigeur,* angry activists with stepladders and
paint-brushes went all down that covered way at the Summer Palace, ex-
punging pictures of un-progressive myth. And tomorrow, when another
generation succeeds to domination, everything may be different again,
and all the values so painstakingly absorbed into the public consciousness
may have to be ripped out of mind once more.

There is a blankness to this despotism. What is it? Who is it? Is it the
people we see on the TV news, smiling benevolently at visiting delegates,
or is it scoundrels out of sight? Is it noble at heart, or rotten? Is it genial

Deng Xiaoping, or some up-and-coming tyrant we have never heard of?
If you climb to the top of Jingshan, Coal Hill, the ornamental mount on
which the last of the Ming Emperors hanged himself from a locust tree,
you may look down upon a string of pleasure-lakes. Their northern waters, within the Behai Park, are alive always with pleasure-craft, and
their lakeside walks are always crowded. The southern lakes look dead
and sterile. No rowing-boats skim their surfaces. No lovers take each other's photographs. The buildings on their banks, contained within high
walls, look rich but tightly shuttered, and only occasionally do you
glimpse a big black car snaking its way down to Changan.

This is where that despotism resides. Behind those walls, beside those
silent lakes, the condition of the Chinese is decided, whether by cynical
opportunists shacked up with girls and Japanese electronics, or by sombre
philosophers bent over their calligraphy. The compound is called Zhongnanhai, and if it all looks numb from Jingshan, it must really be full of
gigantic thrust and calculation. Its main entrance is to the south, with
tilted eaves and two great guardian lions. The red flag flies bravely on a
mast outside, and within the gate an inner wall—the "spirit wall" of old
China—is inscribed with the cabalistic text "Serve The People." You cannot see past it, though. Two armed sentries stand there, with two more
watchful over their shoulders. They look distinctly unwelcoming, even to
Foreign Guests, as they stare motionless and expressionless into the street:
and sure enough, when I asked them if I could take a stroll inside Zhongnanhai, they seemed to think not.

−o / o / o−

But anyway Zhongnanhai is only authority for the moment—only a few
years ago it was the private preserve of Mao's widow Jiang Qing, chief
witch of the Gang of Four, and now locked up for ever. Power in Beijing
runs much deeper than that, is endemic to the very existence of the city:
when the summons came to me at last, I knew better where to go.

From the top of Jingshan a dead straight axis runs from north to
south—or as the Chinese always say, from south to north—through the
center of the city. This is the line of Chinese power. It is like one of those
energy-leys the visionaries profess to find in Europe, conveying the earth
force century after century from mountain to megalith. From the pavilion
on the hill it runs steeply down to the entrance of Jingshan Park (posters
of criminals, placards around their necks, stuck up for the public exam-

ple) and over a wide highway, and across that moat where the singers sing at dawn, and through a great flowery gateway, the Gate of Inspired Military Genius, into the Forbidden City of the Emperors.

This is only a museum now, but it retains the numen of absolute command—a walled city in itself, a matchless assembly of palaces, temples, gardens and gazebos for the exaltation of one single man, the only Son of Heaven, the chieftain of China. Marvellous objects litter our path through this fabulous enclave, grimacing lions of gilded bronze, huge sculpted tortoises, incense burners, ancient crinkled rocks. Now the way opens into a noble courtyard, speckled with green grass, now it narrows into a staircase, or passes through some tall gilded hall, or pauses upon a belvedere, or crosses a running stream. Here is the Palace of Heavenly Purity, and here the Palace of Earthly Tranquillity, and here the Hall of Supreme Harmony itself, where surrounded by gold and vermilion, seated on an immense carved throne amidst dimmed lights and incense, the Emperor looked down contemptuously upon the representatives of the rest of humanity, grovelling on the floor below.

But wait! The line goes on. Down the monumental steps—through the Meridian Gate, where the Emperor, reviewing parades of prisoners, decided there and then which should be decapitated—under that Gate of the Heavenly Peace, Tiananmen, which every good Chinese would wish to see before he dies—and suddenly the prospect opens into a plaza a hundred times, a thousand times as big as anything the Manchus knew. It is the forum of the new China, Tiananmen Square, the greatest square on earth, where an army could be massed, where all the kites in the world could fly, where a million people can gather to cheer their leaders upon the gateway balcony, and stare with curious awe at the 20,000 Elders massed in their grandstands upon the northern side.

Nothing, not even in Beijing, is quite so utterly concrete as Tiananmen Square. Across it Changan runs mercilessly east and west, on each side of it are monstrous buildings in the Revolutionary Heroic manner, all columns and swollen symmetry—the Museum of History on the east, on the west the Great Hall of the People, which was built by 25,000 laborers in ten months, and is bigger than all the buildings of the Forbidden City put together. In the center of the Square towers the obelisk of the People's Heroes Monument; at the southern end, immense but squat, there stands the four-square Mausoleum of Mao Zedong, looking back in vindication past obelisk and Great Hall to the gate from which, on October 1, 1949, Mao himself, the Great Helmsman, proclaimed the new Heaven and the new Earth. Morose sentries stand guard at each corner of this tomb, wearing sandals or baseball shoes, there are gigantic sculpted panels of peasants resurgent, soldiers victorious, and inside, behind a towering effigy of himself, Mao lies in a crystal coffin embalmed, he hopes, for all the ages.

But wait again! The line ends not with Mao Zedong! Past the mausoleum, through the Qianmen Gate, straight as a die the power-force flows through the Outer City to the Temple of Heaven in the south. Three times a year, in old Peking, the Emperor journeyed to this holy place to communicate with his only superiors, the gods themselves. All windows were shuttered for his passing, and the city was plunged in silence: and though we ourselves can take a No. 116 bus down there (try not to hang on to the safety bars—they leave your hands all brown) still a mighty suggestion of celestial collusion awaits us there as it awaited him. After sundry rites and sacrifices in the temple complex it was his duty to ascend the Circular Mound, built in arcane configurations of the number nine, there to seal the intimate association between this city and the ultimate source of all authority, Destiny itself.

We will do the same. Up those terraces we go, to the wide round platform at the top, and on the slab in the very center we will stand like the Son of Heaven before us, and speak aloud to the gods. "All Power is Illusion!" we may impertinently choose to cry: and instantly, by some eerie manipulation of the acoustics, we find ourselves surrounded by the sound of it—*Power, Power, Power, Illusion, Illusion!*—embracing us within the echo of our own thoughts, and making us feel that we really do stand at the bottom of a cylinder reaching directly, from that stone on the mound in Beijing, China, to the Emperor or Chairman of all things.

—o / o / o —

Dazzled, bewildered, profoundly affected, all at once, I retreated from the Chinese presence. Some of those caterpillars on the Great Wall, I had noticed, never make it to the other side, but settle in crannies among the paving: and from there if all goes well, I suppose, they turn themselves into butterflies, and flutter away into the empyrean from the very substance of China. I felt rather like them when the time came for me to leave, for I took the advice the Bureaucrat had given me, and floated my way out through those humped green mountains of Guangxi, away in the humid south.

My two cities of China had left me hazed with conflicting emotions and contradictory conclusions, and like a sleep-walker I wandered back towards the coast. I bicycled down dusty lanes through fecund communes, where laboring girls waved and laughed beneath their comical hats, as in propaganda posters. I clambered precipitous hillocks to take jasmine tea in faery huts. I joined the great daily migration of the tourists down the Li River, stretched out flat in the front of the boat, eating lychees all the way, drifting through a fantasy of bulbous mountains, and green, green paddy-fields, and dragon-flies, and ferry-men, and riverside villages clouded in the song of crickets, and cormorant fishermen squatting on bamboo rafts, and junks punted upstream by women bent agonizingly double at their poles, and geese in the shallows, and peasants high on rock tracks, and water-buffalos snuffling, and old river steamers panting and thumping, while the lychees got steadily squashier in the sun, and the sad man beside me, erect in the prow, bared his chest in the breeze and sailed through those legendary landscapes singing the proud songs of his revolutionary youth.

And so I came out of the heart of China back to the sea once more. I had found no absolutes after all. I had found nothing immutable. I had met a people as confused as any other. I had seen marvellous things and miserable, I had eaten pickled turnip with Mrs. Wang and been sent packing by the sentries of Zhongnanhai. I had been cured of headache by Chinese Wolfberry. I had successfully evaded the Chinese opera. I had bought a bamboo goat, and beaten Mr. Lu at checkers in the park. I had visited the grand simplicities of my imagination, and found them grand indeed, but muddled. I had reached that mighty presence at last, and it was smiling nervously.

Out on the Pearl River, surrounded by black sampans, the ship lay waiting.

Epilogue

So I strand you on the banks of a Chinese river, wondering if there is room in that ship for you: but though you might think it an uncomfortably inconclusive end to a book of journeys, it has a true finality for me. I leave you here. For better or for worse this is my fifth book of collected travel essays, and with it I bring to fulfillment a jejeune ambition—to have seen and described, before I died, the whole of the urban world. Beijing and Shanghai were my last great cities. I may go upstream now instead, or strike into the mountains.

Goodbye then! Good luck! Hope you get a cabin!